ADVENTURES IN RESILIENCE

ADVENTURES IN RESILIENCE
IGNITE THE 12 POWERS IN YOU TO CREATE A RADIANT LIFE

Sharon Connors

Unity Village, MO 64065-0001

Unity Books are available at special discounts for bulk purchases for study groups, book clubs, sales promotions, book signings, or fundraising. To place an order, call the Unity Customer Care Department at 816-251-3571 or email wholesale *accts@unityonline.org*.

Some scripture was taken from the New King James Version. Copyright © 1982 by Thomas Nelson, Inc. Used by permission. All rights reserved.

Some scripture quotations are from the New Revised Standard Version Bible, copyright © 1989 National Council of the Churches of Christ in the United States of America. Used by permission. All rights reserved worldwide.

Cover design: Mark Szymanski

Interior design: Perfection Press

ISBN: 978-0-87159-405-6

Library of Congress Control Number: 2020940848

Canada BN: 13252 0933 RT

Dedication

To Unity, a spiritual path that brought me out of the cloud of unknowing and into the light of a design for living that has made all the difference.

To my parents, John and Cecile Connors, whose remarkable resilience coaxed me forward by being a constant example of it.

To my children, Ed and Jennifer, the lights of my life and joy of my soul, who inspire me with their own resilience.

Table of Contents

Part Three: The Empowered Life

Introduction

Resilience is rooted in a tenacity of spirit—a determination to embrace all that makes life worth living, even in the face of overwhelming odds. When we have a clear sense of identity and purpose, we are more resilient because we can hold fast to our vision of a better future.

—*Wisdom Commons, an interactive web project for parents and educators*

Resilience: ability to recover readily from illness, depression, adversity, or the like; buoyancy.

—*Dictionary.com*

Resilience: an ability to recover from or adjust easily to misfortune or change.

—*Merriam-Webster's Collegiate Dictionary*

Radiance: light or heat as emitted or reflected by something.

—*Oxford Dictionary of English*

Radiance: glow, happiness, delight, joy, brightness, luminosity.

—*Collins Thesaurus of the English Language*

L ack of power—that was my dilemma. No matter how much I tried to change my husband, I was never successful. In fact, the more I failed, the harder I tried. It left me feeling incompetent and frustrated. All of this led to anger turned inward. I felt utterly powerless to manage myself and my life. My own inner resources seemed to fail me. That began to change when a friend introduced me to a spirituality that offered a path to a new kind of power—spiritual power. That is what this book is about.

Even before coming to terms with feeling powerless, I was on shaky ground. As a freshman at Michigan State University, I had felt so overwhelmed with my studies and so afraid of failure that standing naked in front of my dorm room window in zero-degree weather seemed like the best option. I reasoned that catching pneumonia would provide a way out of the darkness I was experiencing. I didn't catch pneumonia, as it turned out, and had to find something in me that was greater than my fear of failure and rapidly progressing despondency. It actually took years of research and experimentation before I came to realize I needed *spiritual* power to provide me with the kind of resilience I was searching for.

Finding a spiritual path that taught me there is a spark of divinity within me and everyone threw many of my long-held spiritual beliefs into a tailspin. My *modus operandi* had been to pray to a God I did not trust. I would placate and make deals with this God, trying to make life and people be the way I wished they would be. I went to support groups, read self-help books, and complained to friends. I prayed and prayed for a solution. How ironic that my fierce struggle with power, my own and God's as it turned out, led to my immersion in the study of 12 capacities that could be spiritualized into sustainable resilience and true power. As I began to study these powers, my whole attitude and outlook on what is possible for human beings began to shift—like the Earth's tectonic plates.

This book shares a map of that spiritual technology and offers simple yet reliable tools to negotiate that journey. It is a map that transcends religious dogma and denominations. Its roots are ancient and transdenominational. It is a spirituality for the twenty-first century.

In her book *Anatomy of the Spirit*, Caroline Myss notes, "When I was still new to intuition, I had not yet made the connection between disease, healing, and personal power, but I now believe that power is the foundation of health."

She explains, "I believe that our cell tissues hold the vibrational patterns of our attitudes, our belief systems, and the presence or absence of an exquisite energy frequency or 'grace' that we can activate."

My purpose in this book is to share a spiritual technology that activates this exquisite energy frequency that is divine in nature, while at the same time being inherent to our human nature.

There are 12 creative powers that are fundamental to each of us. They are aspects of the nature of the Divine. Understanding the true potential of these creative energies and how to engage their power in our lives leads to living a richly blessed life. Donald Meichenbaum, Ph.D., one of the founders of cognitive behavior therapy, has studied the nature of resilience and how to develop it in young people who had been exposed to violence in their homes. He states, "Resilience is the process of adapting well in the face of adversity, trauma, tragedy, threats, or significant sources of stress ... Resilience involves behaviors, thoughts, and accompanying feelings that can be *nurtured, developed,* and *learned.*" The 12 powers that you'll read about in the coming pages give you a way and a practice to evolve your natural-born resilience into radiant presence and character.

With practice, our inherent spiritual capacities mature so that we intuitively know how to handle baffling and difficult circumstances that invariably wash up on the shores of our lives. I found that as I meditated on and acted from these 12 spiritual capacities, I didn't get as emotionally tripped up by what others did or didn't do, said or didn't say. I found that I became more aware of the choice before me: to give my power away to people, places, and things or not. I came to understand that my mind is my link to God through these 12 capacities: wisdom, love, strength, faith, imagination, order, understanding, will, power, zeal, release, and life itself.

In almost 30 years as a minister, I've witnessed people's lives transformed as a result of discovering the spiritual power this book describes. It's a power that is greater than their difficulties, disappointments, distrust, and discouragement. It is a power that can trump worries and fears and dissolve resentments. It is a spiritual power we all have. Truthfully, though, I spent most of my life with no clue that this spiritual power resided in me and in everyone. Instead, I was raised to believe that God, the one power, was outside of me. If I wanted any kind of help, well, I had to be really good, pray right, and do right, and maybe I would get some divine response.

Consequently, I spent most of my life in well-disguised fear. Given that, you can imagine how hungry I was to find an antidote. This book *is* that antidote.

I've done my share of counseling people who felt powerless to manage their emotions and the circumstances in which they found themselves. Counting solely on our human power yields very mixed results.

Even though many of us believe we have to figure it all out on our own, the truth is that we are not alone. We don't have to figure it all out on our own. There is a spark of divinity within us that can be ignited. The result will be a small, steady increase of freedom from fear because, as science has discovered, the "hard drive" of your mind can be reprogrammed.

I was on my way to being reprogrammed one Sunday morning, feeling utterly hopeless and powerless in my marriage. Hysterical and in tears, I called a friend. She suggested I meet her at her church, a Unity church. Right away that was a challenge because, being Catholic, my husband, two children, and I went to Mass on Sundays. I was desperate, however. My friend met me and marched us both up to the third row from the front. I can't remember exactly what the minister said except that a divine presence in me could and would help me. Hope dawned. I had encountered a spiritual belief system that was positive and practical. I wanted more and began to show up every Sunday. I took every class offered and before long came across the 12 powers you will read about in the following pages.

It seems that everyone is feeling afraid these days. Watch the news any day of the week and you will realize we are being called to find a new kind of resilience. While the world confronts global terrorism, widespread illness, and economic upheaval, and we in the United States also experience mass shootings and unprecedented gun violence, our human resilience is intensely tested. We are called to affirm our connection to the divine spark within us through a higher level of thinking, a level that the 12 spiritual powers offer.

I can only compare the experience of studying and practicing the 12-power system with the one and only time I witnessed a full display of the northern lights. Each hot, humid summer in Chicago, when my sisters, brother, and I were kids, my mom and dad would herd the four of us into the car for our much-anticipated vacation in Wisconsin. The year I remember best was our two weeks in a three-bedroom log cabin at Cabot Lodge on Sturgeon Bay. The Dulmas family occupied the cabin next to ours. The three Dulmas children matched my two sisters and me in age (my younger brother had to hang out with us girls).

We had great adventures exploring the rocky cliffs of Potawatomi State Park, just a short rowboat ride across a harbor. Still, none of our adventures could compare to that magical evening when our two families sat outside our cabins, relaxing after a delectable dinner of freshly caught northern pike. Suddenly, the sky opened before us and a gigantic curtain of shimmering green light unfurled. I learned this was the aurora borealis.

To say it was a spectacular, astounding, and inspiring display of power and light doesn't even come close. The shimmering light fell to the earth, spreading its emerald radiance as far as I could see.

Yet that extraordinary display of light pales next to the display of divine power that can be displayed in shades of beauty and mastery in a human life. That radiance lives in each of us. It is a power to thrive no matter what our conditions or circumstances. As hard as it may be to believe, especially if you are suffering deeply right now, you can have a full, rich, meaningful life, free from self-limiting ideas. With the help of our 12 innate powers, we discover that we are more than resilient, and our presence and character radiate with possibility.

This book is about the universal urge to grow, to find the outer reaches of ourselves and what's possible. The 12 soul powers I discovered in Unity provide a perfect vehicle. To be sure, the concept of specific ways that the Divine expresses in and through human beings exists in other faith traditions and philosophies as well. Other faiths have discerned inner powers that are remarkably more than human power alone. Buddhists speak of the Buddha nature and higher Self. Hindus speak of emanations of the One as specialized divine capacities.

Unity cofounder Charles Fillmore, who was strongly influenced by the renaissance thinking during the 1800s referred to as the Transcendental movement, went on a committed spiritual search himself. It led him to Eastern spirituality, which he integrated with the spirituality of his upbringing in Christianity to create the 12-power system. Based on the reality of the divine spark within all people, he used the disciples of Jesus as exemplars of the 12 powers. The system provides a deep, direct connection with the Divine that is realized as the power of resilience, even radiance.

Imagine a peace that surpasses all understanding, a joy that cannot be taken from you, and the ability to walk with grace, as Jesus did, atop any turbulent waters of life. Imagine no fear—at least none that stops you. What would you be doing? What would you be feeling and experiencing? Imagine in times of trouble feeling as if you have the support of divine guidance instead of drowning in the universal, almost automatic response of doubt, worry, or fear. For example, you could turn to your spiritually awakened power of *release* to erase your self-limiting thoughts and beliefs. Imagine feeling supported like that—never alone.

The notion that each of us holds the Divine within us, that we have a spiritual nature along with our humanity, is not new. But most of us don't have a method for developing our spiritual capacities.

The 12 powers provide a system for soul growth, a spiritual system for creating a life that is, as the apostle Paul said, no longer storm-tossed by the difficulties of life and challenges to your faith. The work forms a reliable foundation for developing our fullest potential while creating a life that is meaningful, fulfilling, and contributory. In my own life, it was these 12 capacities that gave me a way out of the utter despair of a failing marriage that was affecting my children and our lives in destructive ways. The search for a new way generated a journey that led me into ministry. Now some 30 years later, my passion for all that these powers are and can do as expressions of the Divine brought me to share this adventure in building resilience.

"Aging Strong" is a relatively new term and current focus of some health-care systems. Studies are being conducted to determine the factors that contribute to staying vibrantly alive as we age. The studies dispel the notion of automatic and unstoppable decline. The researchers find that spirituality inspires purpose, being optimistic, and engaging socially. A committed spiritual practice results in being spiritually fit—and astonishingly resilient.

Aging Strong could be applied to the outcome of engaging the 12 powers. It's a quest for a lifetime. Be reassured, though, that it's about progress and not perfection. Even Mother Teresa had to admit she couldn't always live up to her spiritual potential. Nevertheless, she pursued her magnificent purpose, demonstrating remarkable resilience well into her later years.

Like Mother Teresa and all who want to excel at what they value and are passionate about, practice yields rewards. With practice, you will begin to notice stunning changes in your way of perceiving. Your changes in attitude and outlook will be gradual until you suddenly notice that you are not the same person. You are surprisingly freer and more joyful. You find a purpose worth living from. You notice that you are more optimistic. Contributing to others becomes important and adds zest to your life. You live with a strength that will astonish you.

In his book *Prosperity*, Charles Fillmore, speaking of the 12 powers, says:

> You will find first that your ideas have broadened immensely, that your little limited world has been transformed into a big world. You will find your mind

more alert, and you will see clearly where you were in doubt before ... The consciousness of an omnipotent hand guiding all your affairs will establish you in confidence and security ... There will be a lessening or entire absence of prejudice and faultfinding in you. You will be more forgiving and more generous and will not judge harshly. Other people will feel that there has been a change in you and will appreciate you more, showing it in many ways. Things will be coming your way, being added unto you indeed according to the promise.

That may sound too good to be true, but Fillmore knew it firsthand because of his own experience digging deep for resilience while raising three boys, caring for an ailing wife who had been diagnosed as terminal, and dealing with his own precarious health issues and pending bankruptcy. He needed a solution and found a spiritual one. I figured if it worked for Fillmore, it could work for everybody—including doubting Thomas me.

In her book *Mindset: The New Psychology of Success* (Ballantine Books, 2016), Carol S. Dweck, Ph.D., a world-renowned psychologist at Stanford University, observes that the world is not divided into weak or strong, success or failure, but into learners and nonlearners. Mindsets change what people strive for or don't strive for. A learner mindset is resilient in the face of challenges. Those with a learner mindset persist in challenges. They don't get discouraged by mistakes and delays. In fact, they become more highly motivated. With a learner mindset, you'll discover that the 12 powers will reveal themselves to you.

Spiritual skills can be cultivated just as physical and intellectual skills can be. What if you were to think of these 12 powers as spiritual muscles? Imagine what might happen if you apprenticed yourself to making them strong, resilient, and vibrant. You might not let turbulent emotions and situations get the best of you. You might not let fear stop you. You might make wiser decisions and follow your dreams more readily. You will find yourself not only resilient but there will be a radiance about you that others will identify as peace and joy.

I think of the 12 powers as "inner mansions." You will read about how they work and how to work with them. Each has a vibrational frequency that is both healing and life-giving.

On a practical level, developing these attributes improves our self-image and relationships, and regenerates the body—we become healthier all around!

It isn't necessary to study the powers in order. Choose one that seems to fit the circumstance in which you find yourself. For example, if you are angry with someone, you could turn to the powers of release and love. You would release the anger to the divine presence in you and pray for the person you are angry with. You would be willing to forgive and be open to compassion.

Many years ago, I dared to be a Mary Kay beauty consultant. I say "dared" because of my outrageous fear of rejection. Of all the sales training I received, one of the most helpful was a mantra from Mary Kay Ash: "Consistency is the key to success." I find that idea to be true with any endeavor, including building spiritual muscle and maximizing the possibilities of our spiritual potential.

My hope and prayer is that you are fired up to experiment with expressing the spiritual energy of these 12 powers and the skills they build. You will find a whole new level of trust in yourself, the God of your understanding, and life in general.

A final note: I refer to God in a number of ways—Higher Power, One Power, Source, Creative Energy, the Divine, Spirit. I think of God in those ways myself and hope using a variety of names makes this material perhaps more accessible, whatever your beliefs.

Part One
True Power

Chapter 1
Resilience: An Inherent Power

The alchemists maintained that we can create only in our own image ...
It is essential then, to know what is vital and alive inside us and shape
our lives in its image.

—David Whyte, *The Heart Aroused*

I t was an early afternoon when Jason eased his pickup truck into the driveway alongside his father's 1940s white frame house. He knew his dad would be at work. He needed for his dad to be out of the house. He let himself in with the key his father kept under the mat at the front door and went directly to the gun cabinet in the dining room. He grabbed one of his father's four hunting rifles and left the way he had come in.

Back in his truck, he squealed out of the driveway, spun around, and peeled away. Just as he had planned, as he raced down the road, it didn't take long before he could hear the sirens and see the flashing lights in his rearview mirror.

He led the police into the countryside just outside of Lee's Summit, Missouri. He held the pedal to the metal for a few miles then stopped suddenly. Three police cars circled around him. After being told a few times to get out of the car with his hands raised, Jason opened the door and jumped out with his rifle aimed at the officers standing outside their cars. Shots rang out and Jason slumped to the ground. He had fired no shots. In fact, the police discovered the rifle was not loaded. His death was ruled a suicide. He was 19 years old.

It was a sunny Saturday in October when I officiated at his memorial service. I remember the framed photograph his mom brought in. It must have been one of his high school yearbook pictures. There he was, blond hair, blue eyes, soft smile, and radiating a kind of innocence.

What self-image shaped him and led him to take his life? What happened to his hopes and dreams? Growing up, he loved sports, especially baseball. He was a handsome young man who, in so many ways, seemed to have a lot going for him. Yet by the time he turned 19, he had given up on life and his dreams.

Langston Hughes, poet, activist, and playwright, wrote a poem about the resilience factor:

> Hold fast to dreams
> For if dreams die
> Life is a broken-winged bird
> That cannot fly.
>
> Hold fast to dreams
> For when dreams go
> Life is a barren field
> Frozen with snow.

Jason's dreams appeared to have died. Somewhere in his young life, the resilience factor in him clouded over until he couldn't find it anymore. Maybe he didn't realize he had it in him. Drugs served as his resilience, until they didn't. He had put his faith in them rather than the divine spark in him. The drugs proved to be a false friend.

The resilience factor is in all of us as an expression of life itself. It is our capacity to move from being a victim to a survivor and then to a thriver. From a physician's perspective, best-selling author Larry Dossey said he believes, "Resilience is built into life itself. It requires a kind of toughness, the ability to recover quickly from difficult situations, and must take place within a set of moral, ethical, and spiritual standards."

That describes my mom. She loved to go shopping in downtown Chicago. However, just as important to her was her favorite spiritual watering hole. She always made a visit to St. Peter's in the Loop a part of her excursion. She also liked to take me along with her. I didn't much enjoy the shopping part, but our visit to St. Peter's church was a magical experience.

From the outside you would never guess that the inside could be as magnificent as it was. The church was tucked, wall to wall, between two retail shops on West Madison Street. You really had to know where you were going or you would definitely miss it. Ah, but once you entered, it was breathtaking even for a preteen like me.

I say all this because even at 11 years old I felt inexplicable peace and safety once inside. There were soaring, vaulted ceilings, frescoed walls, and banks of flickering votive candles standing before statues of saints that lined both sides of the sanctuary, some in shadowed alcoves. Two long rows of Italian marble columns, separated by a wide center aisle, led to the main altar, which was arrayed with fresh flowers. On either side of the altar were crimson-clad thrones with golden arms and legs. A faint scent of incense from the morning Mass hung in the air. Even as a youngster, I felt a soothing, calming sensation that, oddly enough, energized me. All my senses stood in awe, and my thoughts were somehow cleansed of an as-yet-unnamed fear.

That was a counterpoint, actually, to my young interpretation of the God of my religious education—that God might love me, but only if I were good. If I wasn't good, there was no telling what horrible fate might befall me. Meanwhile, my understanding of *good* was definitely not my own. In the Catholic grade school and high school I attended, there were all kinds of spoken and unspoken rules about what was good and what was sinful. Each set seemed to threaten my existence. I yearned for a trusting, intimate relationship with the God I didn't understand at all back then— one in which I felt safe, like I felt at St. Peter's. It has been quite a long and winding road to find that God, one that I can trust with everything—most of the time, that is.

In the pages ahead, you'll read about the God I found after all my searching. The God I came to understand is the creative principle/law/energy of the universe. While God is the great mystery that can never be fully grasped by our human intelligence, God can be perceived through experience and through a passionate effort to form an intimate, trusting relationship.

Braedon seemed to know about this kind of relationship at a very young age. He loved to go to church with his mom—my daughter—and his dad. One Sunday morning, at a mere 5 years old, Braedon walked away from his parents, who always sat in the fourth-to-last row in the sanctuary. As they slid into their usual row of chairs, Braedon marched to the second row from the front and found a seat. My daughter and Braedon's dad, John, along with his two older brothers, quickly followed and found seats with him. Asked why he insisted on coming to the front, Braedon said, "I want to be close to Jesus." He echoed what we all feel at some point in our lives—an internal yearning to have a trusting, intimate relationship with a power greater than ourselves. Something in us reaches out to the Great Mystery, and the truth is, as a wave is part of the ocean, we are a part of this Great Mystery, the One God called by many names.

There are five spiritual principles that form a foundation for encountering such a God and entering into a study of the 12 powers. These five principles include keys for life mastery. They are tools for bringing the 12 powers to their fullest expression.

The first principle is to come to believe in God as the creative principle of life; God as the energy and manifestation of love; goodness itself; the substance of all that is; power, principle, intelligence, wisdom, source energy, mind, and being.

The second principle is that we are individualized expressions of the One. The divine spark is part and parcel of our DNA. Within us abides the fire of life. This means we can directly access this power. The implications assure us of our own inherent power of resilience and our yearning to explore the outer reaches of this resilience—an inner radiance.

The third principle is the good news and the bad news. The good news is that we create our experience by our thoughts. That is also the bad news. We create our reality by our thoughts, whatever they are. Our thoughts can free us or imprison us. What we think about becomes our current reality and, if continued, our destiny. The key spiritual skill to develop is staying awake to our thoughts and changing them if we see that they will not make us happy.

The fourth principle contains the tools for transformation of consciousness while developing a healing, heartwarming, soul-satisfying relationship with a God who is personal to us. There are four tools: prayer and meditation; denial and affirmation. Denial is our spiritual eraser. It is our "no-saying" power. Affirmation is our artistry. It is our "yes-saying" power to all that is good and beautiful, helpful and healing. Both activities happen to be two of our 12 spiritual powers. Denial is our power of elimination. Affirmations express our power of faith.

A denial can be as simple as saying *no* to a thought that is not helpful. Affirmations, on the other hand, are statements of what you want to bring into your life. You will see examples of affirmations, sometimes combined with denials, at the end of each chapter.

Finally, the fifth principle reminds me of Oscar Hammerstein's idea that a bell is not a bell until you ring it. The fifth principle asks us to metabolize the first four by endeavoring to live from them to the best of our ability in every arena of our lives—health, work, money, relationships, creative expression, and enjoyment—on the highways, in the grocery store, during telephone conversations, at dinner parties, and at the office.

These five principles empower your 12 powers because you have immediate access to the One Power, the creative principle of Goodness itself. The divine is part of who you are. The challenge, of course, is in living from this fact. The third principle, the creative law, gives you not only the choice to create your reality but the responsibility as well. The key is to use the tools of transformation, your *yes* and *no* power, to take charge of your thinking. You can, for example, focus on seeking divine guidance when you don't know what to do. You could ask yourself, *What would love do?* instead of fighting back when hurt. The fifth principle invites you into practice. How might you embody the powers of love or strength or faith?

It was an unusually warm, sunny day as my friend David and I left San Francisco early to get across the Bay Bridge. We were on our way to see His Holiness, the Dalai Lama. He would be speaking at the University of California, Berkeley. Anticipating a huge crowd, we wanted to be sure we could get good seats at the enormous Greek Theatre on campus.

After negotiating the ever-heavy traffic on the Bay Bridge, we followed the lines of cars into the parking lot at the university. We scrambled across campus ahead of the crowd and found great seats in the center of the amphitheater some 15 rows up. The crystal clear blue sky, gentle breeze, and April warmth made it a perfect day for the Dalai Lama's speech and for being outside. David had thought ahead to bring stadium cushions for us to sit on, especially since we had a 40-minute wait until the Dalai Lama took the stage. Even on a nice day, the semicircle cement seating was chilly.

As the rows of seats filled, the air became electrified with high-voltage excitement and anticipation. Finally, the attending dignitaries began to take their places on the stage. A petite, dark-haired woman stepped to the microphone. She spoke of the Dalai Lama's work to establish peace in the world and then outlined his many accomplishments and acts of courage. A hush fell on the crowd as she began her introduction of the spiritual icon we had all come to see. When she said, "And, now, ladies and gentlemen, please welcome His Holiness, the Dalai Lama," everyone spontaneously jumped up and began cheering as he came into view in his crimson and orange robes. I'm sure the thunderous applause and shouts could be heard all the way across the Bay to San Francisco.

An aide escorted him up the three steps to the stage and over to the microphone. Everyone stood in honor as he slowly made his way. As the crowd took its seats, a huge smile spread across the Dalai Lama's face and he began to speak in Chinese, his first language. He went on for a few minutes. David and I looked at each other puzzled. Suddenly, he burst into laughter. With a big grin, he spoke out in clear English, "Surprised you!" We all cheered. Then he spent the next hour talking in English about the importance of love, forgiveness, compassion, and doing our part to create peace and a world that works for everyone.

Here is a man who evidently has found and maximized the light in him to such an extent that others can come to believe in the light in themselves. He speaks simply of the complex work of developing our own spiritual power. He spoke of the arduous work of transcending our human fears and resentments; of the urgency in these times to make of our lives a work of art that helps create peace among all people, even in the face of differences in religion, politics, culture, color, and orientation.

It occurred to me that this is going to require what the Big Book of Alcoholics Anonymous calls a complete psychic change. It is no easy task to maintain peace of mind and heart. His Holiness admitted that he has had his moments! However, he has managed to make of himself a light, and if one person can do it, we all can. His radiance of being has inspired so many others to let go of the notions that separate us in order to make personal and global peace possible. He lives the idea of keeping a focus on solutions rather than problems.

The radiance that shines in the Dalai Lama is a seed in each of us. It yearns for our attention to develop it. It thrives on our faith in it. The divine spark is bigger than all our doubts, worries, and fears. It ignites our thinking with inspiring thoughts and spiritually nourishing ideas.

It is true that life tests us over and over. It asks, *Will you surrender your power or ignite the light in you?* I remember evangelist Robert Schuller saying, "If you've got a problem, good. God will provide a way around it, over it, or through it." As you focus on igniting the light of God within you, expressing as the 12 powers, you will keep your divine battery well-charged while empowering yourself to be a solution finder. It is a spiritual fitness program that clears the way for your resilience to grow into radiance.

AFFIRM

- *I release my fears to God, and God in me gives me courage and guidance.*

- *Step-by-step, the light of God in me sets me free to be all I can be.*

- *I am open and receptive to knowing and living from the divine power in me.*

PRAY

Most amazing Spirit, I now immerse myself in your light within me. With every breath, I breathe your light into every part of me. You light my mind with right choices. Mighty currents of your presence in me minister to me in every needed and desired way. In the quiet, I listen for your still, small voice guiding my thoughts and my steps.

PRACTICE

1. Write the above affirmations on a card and say each three times a day. Notice any changes in you and/or the way your day goes.

2. Each morning and from time to time during the day, envision a radiant light in your heart. As you focus on this vision in your mind's eye, see it brighten, expand, and radiate like the sun throughout your whole body. Notice your energy in doing this.

3. Take time this week, and now as you read, to reflect on the ways and times you have demonstrated resilience—

for example, times when you have come back from loss, hurt, or disappointment; times when you have wanted to give up on something important to you but didn't. Here's the thing: A mind once stretched can't go back to what it was. You own a capacity once grown—it's yours.

Chapter 2
Radiance: A Developed Power

Within each person there is a new world awaiting discovery, a world in which there are capabilities of unlimited strength, perfect knowing, radiant life, and other latent abilities beyond our greatest present capacity to conceive.

—Winifred Wilkinson Hausmann, *Your God-Given Potential*

Now the Lord is the Spirit, and where the Spirit of the Lord is, there is freedom. And we all, with unveiled face, beholding the glory of the Lord, are being changed into his likeness from one degree of glory to another ...

—2 Corinthians 3:17-18 (RSV)

My tennis friend, Joan, told me I really needed to meet her friend Peggy. She gave me Peggy's phone number, assuring me, "You will just love her. You two are both into spiritual things." That captured my interest right away. Then when Joan added, "She has written a book on prayer," I could hardly wait to call her. I had been puzzling over a title and perspective to take on this book and hoped our conversation would help me make a choice.

It was a brilliant, warm day in San Diego when I met Peggy at Panera Bread. As I approached the front door, I noticed a woman sitting on the Panera patio. I knew it had to be Peggy because when our eyes met, her face lit up with a beautiful, welcoming smile.

When she asked, "What do you want to write about?" I heard myself say, "Hope. I think the world needs hope." She agreed. We talked for a bit about the reasons—global violence, rampant fear of terrorist attacks, unprecedented suicides, the spreading current of cynicism, the ubiquitous expressions of hostility, anger, and intolerance—and that was before the COVID-19 pandemic. "The hope the world needs now," I commented, "is that there is a power in us greater than all of the painful, disturbing, and discouraging circumstances we see or face." I said, "I want my book to give readers hope. It's about how God can be expressed in and through us in 12 ways. These 12 powers have been a source of hope for me since I first heard of them more than 25 years ago when I most needed their positive energy and a promise to be out of pain." Peggy agreed, "That's what I hope for in the prayer group I lead. I want people to believe in the power of God to help them deal with whatever they are going through." If you have ever overcome a difficulty in your life, you've demonstrated the energy of hope.

To pray with hope is like the father in scripture who brought his son with epilepsy to Jesus (Mark 9:23 NKJV) with hope the boy could be healed: "Lord, I believe; help my unbelief!" In other words, "Give me the kind of hope that is grounded in faith, one that is resilient in times of trouble." The seed of resilience is the energy of faith-filled hope that can be developed into unshakable faith, the kind the man with the epileptic son prayed for. It is the radiant light that guides your way to divine right action.

Something in us jumps for joy at the thought of living with no limits. My favorite instructor when I was in seminary at Unity Village, Rev. Marvin Anderson, would say, "This is the whole secret, folks" as he spoke of the 12 powers. He said, "After many years of study and research, I settled on this system of the mystical 12." He went on, "This is the most valuable and, perhaps, the most useful system for spiritual growth. It has no rival." It was then that I committed to explore the 12 powers system.

The journey to wholeness is to find the treasures of the kingdom of heaven, the inner mansions, which these 12 powers open to us, and then develop them to their fullest potential. The treasures we find are gifts that we can bring as inspiring character qualities to our world. We become powerful instruments in healing the world because we have healed our own heart and soul. We develop the capacity to be a healing presence in the lives of others. For example, the power of love in its spiritualized expression becomes compassion rising out of true forgiveness and humility. Compassion begets kindness. Love is not limited to those who are easy to love.

When I was living in San Francisco, colleagues introduced me to the work of Brian Swimme. He is a renowned cosmologist and professor at the California Institute of Integral Studies in San Francisco. Following their enthusiasm and glowing comments, I signed up for a silent retreat he offered at Dominican University of California, just across the Golden Gate Bridge, sheltered amidst tall pines and gigantic oaks that grace the winding roads of the campus.

He shared his astonishing conclusions about universal energy, saying, "The Universe, God, keeps drawing us in, keeps coming to us and offering life and elegant care." My heart and mind were on fire with that idea. Clearly, for him the universe radiates the wonders of Creativity itself. He urged, "We are now faced with how to use power that does not come from hands. It's about shaping things with an idea." He added, "We need to come to inhabit a deeper creative power." His research convinced him that radiance is one of the powers of the cosmos. He said, "Every object in the universe has the capacity to release light." This is true for each of us human beings as well. Jesus said, "I am the light of the world" (John 8:12), and he said, "You are the light of the world … Let your light so shine before men, that they may see your good works and give glory to your Father who is in heaven" (Matthew 5:14, 16 RSV). In other words, the light of any of these 12 powers shining in and through you helps others find the light in themselves. They will want what you have.

Our life experiences shape our understanding of and relationship with God. Mine was a roller coaster—God is Good; God is punishing; God is love; God is whimsical. It definitely did not build trust. When our backs are to the wall and our own resources are not enough to handle an experience, we tend to call on a power greater than ourselves for help. If we feel helped, our faith grows but is still tenuous and can be fleeting. If we do not feel helped, we tend to increase our efforts or turn away, letting disillusionment drive our choices. The deep yearning to know a God who is greater than our disappointments, that is responsive to our needs, will insist that we not give up. There is something in us that impels us to seek this greater power. It is like an eternal flame deep inside that cannot be extinguished—it may be hidden but not extinguished. What if it is the Divine itself seeking relationship and expression in and through us?

Harriet was a well-known rebirther—a system of breathwork designed to clear and cleanse energy/emotional blocks—in Florida. My friend Sharon and I went through a series of sessions with her, and we both definitely experienced greater aliveness and clarity. Subsequent synchronous events led me to Holotropic Breathwork® with Jack Kornfield, Ph.D., and Stanislav Grof, M.D., at a retreat in Yucca Valley, California. That's where it happened! A young woman at the retreat shared with me that, through toning and meditation, she experienced kundalini energy. Having read about its being a pure state of bliss, I asked whether we could try it together. We found a bright, empty room on the retreat center grounds for the experiment. In the pristine stillness, we sat in meditation, and then Julie, sitting behind me, began to chant around my back, shoulders, and neck. Suddenly, a vibrant pulsing began at the base of my spine. It was as if a veil were wrenched away and the extraordinary love of God began to fill my body. I spontaneously laid back as the energy gushed up to fill me. It seemed to last for hours, but it was only minutes. All sense of time and space disappeared. Bliss! I thought to myself, *This must be the full joy that Jesus and other spiritual masters have spoken of.*

I tell this story because it convinced me that we can access this transforming power. It is the radiance of the Divine shining in and through human beings. In the framework of kundalini yoga, radiance is the result of God uncoiling itself in us. It is the unveiling and release of creative spiritual power in each of us. It lights us up with healing, enlivening energy. It is what Charles Fillmore and the Transcendentalists of the nineteenth century called living in the fourth dimension.

Radiance is a magnetic field of positive energy. It is the divine source in us, radiating outward, dispelling darkness. It is, as the Gospel of John states, the light that shines in the darkness, and the darkness cannot overcome it. It is an experience of oneness with the Divine that generates a unifying energy with the light in all.

Spiritual teachers throughout the ages have spoken of a light that is in every human being. The power inherent in this light can be developed to express something of the nature of God. In fact, it's often referred to as enlightenment. Engaging these creative powers with intention and through disciplined spiritual practice, you will come to live a life with a kind of soul freedom that will astound you. We become a healing presence. The idea is that through dedicated practice and awareness, we metabolize high-frequency creative power. We come to see that our whole life up-levels. We are tapped into the one mind flowing in and through us.

AFFIRM

- *The radiance of Spirit now blesses my thoughts and words and guides my actions.*

- *I am the light of God expressing and blessing my world.*

- *The light of God in me leads me in prospering ways.*

PRAY

I invoke the radiance of God that lives in me, and I set it free by the power of my thoughts. I bathe in the light of God and let it do its perfect work in me now. Thank you, God, for the radiance of your presence in me, inspiring me to all that is good and worthy.

PRACTICE

1. Put the above affirmations in your phone to look at throughout the day.

2. Record the affirmations and listen to them in the morning as you prepare for the day and in the evening before bed.

3. Wherever you are during the day, affirm and see yourself as the light of God expressing in a way that is most helpful at that moment.

Chapter 3
Spiritual Alchemy:
Discover the Power Within You

Truly, I say to you, if you have faith and never doubt, you will not only do what has been done to the fig tree, but even if you say to this mountain, "Be taken up and cast into the sea," it will be done.

—Matthew 21:21 (RSV)

W hen my friend invited me to the Unity church during a very difficult time in my life, I felt a ray of hope flash into my darkness. My starving, fractured soul couldn't get enough of this positive, practical spirituality. I felt hope as if for the first time. I began to believe that what I was experiencing as an insurmountable mountain in my life could be vanquished and cast into the sea of nothingness.

I had been a spiritual seeker for some years. Yet I had hit a wall where my own resources and beliefs were not big enough to handle the pain of an abusive marriage. When I encountered the 12 powers system, it whispered hope into the blinding storms in my heart.

I was captivated by the idea that the 12 disciples of Jesus are spiritual exemplars for 12 creative energies in us, energies that develop along spiritual lines and generate remarkable outcomes. Gradually, my understanding of God began to change—drastically. I began to understand God as the creative energy of the universe, the matrix of all creativity. I began to see the 12 pow-

31

ers as a perfect paradigm in which the 12 disciples were students mentored into being teachers by Jesus, and that I might become a disciple to these powers as well.

This ragtag group of 12 went on to become apostles as a result of mastering the transforming education Jesus provided. Could the divine power in me mentor the 12 "disciples" in me? Like the chakra system in which each creative energy governs the health and well-being of a different organ and physical capacity, the 12 powers govern the health and well-being of our soul and spirit (and, I believe, our body).

In this system, there is a color associated with each power that expresses a unique vibrational frequency in the spectrum of light. The power is seated in a specific area of the body corresponding to the way in which the power functions. For example, love is located in the heart, where blood rightly sent out through our body keeps us alive by nourishing all parts of the body. Spiritually speaking, love expressed in its highest form keeps our whole being vibrantly alive, nourishing all the areas of our lives while it creates a sense of well-being.

Allured by the prospect of such a life, light shone in my darkness. I began to experiment. When I went out for a run, I began to use affirmations for each of the 12 powers as I ran. I would visualize them as lights in my body and breathe their color throughout my body. I thought of this exercise as praying, connecting me to the one power/mind. Did I notice immediate God consciousness? No! But honestly, as the days passed and my practice persisted, my mind seemed to get clearer. My life improved little by little because my thinking improved. I was able to respond more often than react.

Just as we don't have to understand the principles of physics and electricity to enjoy their products, we don't have to know the mystery of the powers to reap the benefits of working with them. I will say this, though: If we reflect on the extraordinary technology of today, we have a metaphor for this invisible spiritual power at work in us. We can trust that when we plug our minds into divine mind, the "electricity"—the power—will flow and our being will be enlightened in specific ways.

Each of the powers has its human aspect and expression. It works like this: Our human faith learns to trust that our mail will arrive at its destination, that the bank will credit our deposit to our account, that our car will get us where we want to go, that the hair dye will turn our hair the color promised. Our understanding gets us through school and mediates our relationships. Yet when these inherent creative capacities are spiritualized, we begin to see through appearances to a deeper truth, a truth that empowers us not to allow circumstances to destroy our peace and joy. We come to trust the light in us to guide us even as we walk into the unknown, even in times of financial uncertainty, even in the midst of loss, difficulty, or disappointment.

Jesus trained his 12 disciples to facilitate the miracles he did and even greater ones. The same is possible for all who disciple themselves to spiritual principles. You could banish any paralyzing fears in your heart, raise deadened dreams to life, or release unfruitful habits and ideas. Spiritual masters across faith traditions have maintained that we all have the power to transform our lives and, in so doing, experience what can only be called miracles.

Jesus and other spiritual masters have pointed to the potential of the light of Spirit within us. It seems that something about the power of light has always been alluring to humankind: the brilliance of the sun rising; the apricot, crimson, yellow, and purple lights of the setting sun; a rainbow of refracted light; a candle burning; the moon hanging in a crystal clear sky. We are drawn to light as though invisible arms reach out to us. Spiritual teachers throughout the ages have spoken of a light in every human being that can be developed to express the nature of the Divine. Enlightenment for all!

Today alternative healing practices are founded on the principle of light as the vibration of the Divine, which can be transmitted through a practitioner to a patient, plant, or energy field. It can affect a shift in energy that is healing or at least helpful.

I ask you to keep an open mind and experiment with these ideas. You'll find affirmations, visualizations, and prayers for each of the powers in the chapters ahead. It's a spiritual practice for a lifetime. The more you practice, the more spiritual power you will develop. The result is that you will intuitively know how to handle situations that used to confound you. You will feel divinely guided beyond anything you could figure out for yourself. You will notice a new synchronicity pervading your life. You will come to see how all your experiences led you forward.

Imagine the creative energy of the universe, God, differentiated in us as 12 capacities that empower us to master circumstances rather than being mastered by them when developed. What Paul said to the Philippians holds true for you: "I can do all things through him who strengthens me" (Philippians 4:13).

With your focused attention and intention to embody their full spiritual essence, these 12 spiritualized powers will equip you to live an incredibly meaningful, impactful, and fulfilling life. One universal truth is that what we focus on increases. Based on that truth, we can increase our spiritual powers by focusing on them. The essence of these powers is light whose vibration is divinely coded.

In his book, *Atom-Smashing Power of Mind*, Charles Fillmore deduced, "The diamond owes its brilliance to the perfect arrangement of the innumerable little prisms within it, each of which refracts the light of the other. Man's body is made up of centers of consciousness—of light—and if arranged so they radiate the light within you, you will shine like the diamond." Point to your heart and say, "This means me!" It describes the spiritual alchemy of the 12 powers.

Alchemy is defined as a power or process that changes something in a mysterious and impactful way. The nature or composition of something is transmuted. In a spiritual sense, doubts and worries can be alchemized into faith—through action. Pessimism becomes optimism. Jealousy is transmuted into self-assurance. Anger becomes forgiveness and right action.

Assigned a Talmudic origin and repeated in the writing of Anaïs Nin, "We don't see things as they are, we see them as we are." Looking through the spiritual lens of any of the 12 powers transforms what seems negative into something helpful and, perhaps, directive.

That happened to Yvette one day, and it changed her life. She grew up in Argenta, Illinois. She was not a very good student. In fact, she didn't like school much at all. Art was the only class she liked because she seemed to have a gift for it. Yet at the end of her sophomore year, she dropped out of school. She worked off and on as a waitress and at 16 married her high school sweetheart. Things were difficult for them. She felt as though something in her had died. Fast-forward from Argenta, Illinois, to La Quinta, California.

I met Yvette at the La Quinta Arts Festival a few years ago. Her art drew me into her stall. Her glass designs were edgy and exquisitely beautiful. I wanted to know more about her and her work.

She said, "I dropped out of high school and was going nowhere fast. One day I ran into my high school art teacher who told me how talented he thought I was. He encouraged me to get back into my art." In this case, her former art teacher performed spiritual alchemy. What he said so touched her heart and soul that she went back to school and began developing the gift of God in her as art. Now an acclaimed artist, no more challenges, right? Wrong. "When I started to work in glass sculpture, experimenting with grinding the glass, I just couldn't get it. I was ready to give up when I heard a voice in me say, 'Try one more time.'" It worked. She apprenticed herself to her gift and to the voice of Spirit within her, and discouragement was alchemized into courage and perseverance.

In the book *Why God Won't Go Away*, Andrew Newberg, M.D., and Eugene d'Aquili, M.D., Ph.D., write on brain science and the biology of belief. They found various key brain structures, and the way information is channeled along neural pathways led to the hypothesis that the brain possesses a neurological mechanism for self-transcendence. Yvette would agree. This kind of spiritual alchemy can work for everyone. Have you marginalized a gift? A dream? A deep heart's desire? Have you been hearing a whisper saying "just do it"—and are you ignoring it?

AFFIRM

- *Spirit in me now reveals my next right steps, and I go forward with confidence.*

- *I let go of my way, quiet my mind, and listen expectantly for God's way.*

- *In prayer, I link my mind with the mind of God in me, and all that I need to know is revealed.*

PRAY

I envision myself bathed in the divine presence in and around me. I open my awareness to the light of God filling every cell and atom of my being. Resting in the light of God in me, I am healed and guided. I am nourished by the peace of God.

PRACTICE

1. Practice being the observer of your thoughts and emotions. Let go of anything negative and refocus on an energizing affirmation.

2. When you don't know what to do or say, let the Divine in you supply the right words and actions.

3. Do something you are afraid to do. Notice what happens on the other side of that action.

Chapter 4

Spiritual Apprenticeship

Apprentice: One who is learning by practical experience under skilled workers a trade, art, or calling.

—Merriam-Webster

Make yourself a door through which to be hospitable, even to the stranger in you.

—David Whyte, "Coleman's Bed"

In his book *The Alchemist*, Paulo Coelho tells the story of a young boy, Santiago, who believes in his very own unique treasure and decides to go search of it. In the process, Santiago discovers his resilience as he meets with difficulties and disappointments and yet does not turn back or give up his search. Along the way, he encounters the alchemist. The alchemist assures Santiago that he is on the right track when he refuses to counsel his doubts. At one point, the alchemist tells the boy that he is leaving because the boy's education in the skills of alchemy is complete. Santiago had successfully apprenticed himself, finding the treasure within.

Santiago's adventures with the alchemist led him to understand the nature of alchemy, the kind of alchemy I'm talking about here. The boy, speaking to the sun, says:

> This is why alchemy exists … so that everyone will search
> for his treasure, find it, and then want to be better than he
> was in his former life …

That's what alchemists do. They show that, when we strive to become better than we are, everything around us becomes better, too.

The true treasure of life is within us. Jesus assured his disciples and listeners of this. It is the divine seed that we have the privilege and the rare challenge to develop into its full, spectacular expression as 12 creative powers.

"The boy reached through to the Soul of the World, and saw that it was a part of the Soul of God. And he saw that the Soul of God was his own soul. And that he, a boy, could perform miracles." I think the Bible, especially the New Testament, is actually a testament to the fact that we, too, have what it takes to effect miracles.

A few years ago, I traveled to Ávila, Spain, with Caroline Myss. Her book, *Entering the Castle,* had recently been published. For the book, Caroline explored the levels that St. Teresa of Ávila had identified in her sixteenth-century book, *The Interior Castle.* As our group walked through the convent that St. Teresa called home, I felt myself enveloped in the energy of radical devotion that St. Teresa practiced. Caroline shared how profoundly she had been transformed by her research. She said it took her to the core of her being and opened her imagination to the faces and phases of the divine presence within. She said she came to believe that everything we do counts and that *blissful* is, as the Buddha said, the accumulation of good. The disciples apprenticed themselves to the teachings of Jesus. He taught them, through demonstration, the art and practice of miracle-working—or creating good.

My friend, Rose, called one night. I could tell right away by the tone of her voice that things with her beloved husband had taken a turn for the worse. Doctors couldn't seem to find a cure for what was making him so sick. He had been diagnosed with pneumonia, but it had gone on now for two months. Instead of improving, his condition was worsening.

They had drawn blood sample after blood sample, stuck tubes down his throat, needles in his back, run test after test with nothing conclusive. Now they were thinking maybe, after all, it might be cancer. Rose needed to vent and, yet, in the midst of her anger and tears, I could hear something so sweet and pure. Deep love and immense strength and undeterred-by-the-facts understanding produced a laser clarity and strength she hadn't realized she had. It's what we all have. Sometimes it takes a heartbreaking experience to discover the well of resilience that lives in each of us. At least, that's what I've experienced. I've also seen it work that way with family members, friends, and plenty of people I've counseled. It seems that we must name our pain and claim it (that is, accept it) before we can do anything about it.

When I first heard the call to ministry, the thought was so frightening that I avoided claiming it totally. Still, it was relentless. I finally surrendered and opened the door of consideration—very reluctantly and fearfully. I shuddered thinking about what I would say to my parents, who were devout Irish Catholics—I mean, crucifixes hanging in clear view, holy cards and prayers on the kitchen windowsill, and saying grace before meals. They would probably disown me. My sisters and brother would, no doubt, think I had gone off the deep end—yet again. My children would be mystified and maybe even embarrassed. Profoundly surprising to me was that the call proved stronger than all those fears. And just as surprising, my family, while baffled, accepted the decision without the remonstrance I feared. That was a miracle right there.

During my two years in Unity seminary, I was reacquainted with Charles Fillmore's system of 12 powers in a way that captivated me. At some level, I understood that endeavoring to embody each of the 12 powers would free me from the fears that I was aware of. It just so happened that *free* has been my favorite word in the English language. I suspect that is because most of my life I felt imprisoned by umpteen fears—failure, rejection, and mistakes. I found myself constantly at the mercy of the people around me, giving my power away at the drop of a hat—or a word, for that matter. The 12 powers held a carrot of hope. Maybe they would be my doorway to freedom from the straitjacket of fears.

As I was growing up in Chicago, on warm summer nights, lightning bugs came out of their hiding places in the trees to roam the earth. The flickering light of these little creatures lured us kids to chase after them. It was a great adventure trying to capture these wonders of nature in the jars my mom found for us. My dad would punch air holes in the jar lids and off we'd go in search of flying light. I would follow their flicker, wishing I could light up at will as they did. When we were lucky enough to enclose a couple of them in our jars, we were up close and personal with the magic light.

Something in us knows there is more to us than meets the eye, that we are meant to shine, maybe even that there is a magic kind of light in us that we can turn on. As I apprenticed myself to these powers, I came to believe the light is actually in us, as Jesus said. Can we, by a devoted study and practice of the 12 powers, be transfigured as Jesus was? I believe we can. I believe I am to bring light to the world I walk in. Isn't that what we are supposed to do with the life we've been given? I believe the more of this inner light we awaken and are guided by, the happier we are.

You can get up close and personal with the divine light in you. In fact, you can, little by little, step-by-step, be the light. Others experience the good energy of our light and discover the same yearning in themselves. I say *light,* but I could say the power of beautiful character as well. I could call it the radiance of our Creator in us making us resilient beyond measure.

An apprentice is committed to mastery and is there day in and day out, rain or shine, to learn and master the skills needed for the art he or she is pursuing. Mastery happens slowly and then suddenly. Think about anything you have learned. You invested time and energy in learning the subject. Maybe it was tedious at first, but then one day you noticed that you could do what you couldn't come close to doing before. It was as if all your efforts suddenly paid off. It works the same way with spiritual principles and practice.

I came to realize this when I moved to San Francisco, thrilled to be the new minister at Unity Spiritual Center, the "cute little church on the corner" of Ocean and 19th Avenue, and took up rollerblading. At first and for quite a while, I was halting and unsteady, tilting from one side to the other as I painstakingly moved forward. My ankles would arc inward toward the blacktop path, and my arms would jump out from my sides to steady the ship as I made my way from Blackie's Pasture to downtown Tiburon. I loved the views across the water to Sausalito and the expansive vista in front of me across San Francisco Bay to the alabaster skyline of the city.

One sunny Sunday afternoon, a year or two into my new hobby, I was skating along to the song I was singing as I tacked from one side of the trail to the other. As if for the first time, I realized that I had become fairly proficient and rollerblading had become pure joy rather than effortful. Like our spiritual practice—at first slowly, then suddenly—we see how we have been changed. It's spiritual alchemy.

Alchemy is energy work. While it transforms, it purifies, matures, and perfects. That's what the alchemist taught Santiago. He taught the boy a new aspect of his inherent power. He referred to it as the boy's treasure and told him it was his destiny to find it. Jesus taught his disciples that the treasure of the kingdom was within them, and it was their destiny to seek and find it. The dynamic, creative energies of the 12 powers do this work on all three levels of our being—spirit, soul, and body.

Fascinated with the idea of alchemy as applied to psycho-spiritual aspects of change, I was introduced to the work of shamans. They wouldn't use the term *alchemy*; they would more likely use the term *shape-shifting* regarding what they do to heal people. Shamans go into an altered state through drumming and chanting, seeking their power animal and higher self. In spiritual practice, we shape-shift our consciousness—beliefs, attitudes, perceptions—by developing our spiritual power. I noticed that my thinking shifted dramatically as I practiced. Old, hold-me-back fears were alchemized (not all of them, maybe, but definitely the grosser ones) into faith. In looking back, the tedious practice of confronting and banishing hardheaded fears was worth it. The rewards for such efforts have included an incisive, fearless mind; a clean, shining heart that attracts great good; an inexplicable sense of freedom; and a positively impactful—and very fun—life.

It is all about discipline—disciplining ourselves to evolve our power into its full spiritual expression. Our internal conversations are either growing us or slowing us. Disciplining our thoughts is like going to the fitness center to work out. It's hard in the beginning. The muscles are lazy, maybe flabby. It takes effort to achieve lift off, but a disciplined workout results in vigor, a fit body, and endorphin production (the joy generator). I think of the 12 powers discipline as a rigorous spiritual workout, much like a fitness center. A disciplined practice results in an enlightened consciousness that makes the body of our life remarkably healthy.

When you work with these powers, you are working with divine energy. This energy has life, substance, and intelligence and knows what to do. We don't have to make it do what we want. We only need to believe in its intelligence and efficacy. Our part is to give each power grateful and loving attention, and it will go to work in us and for us.

These divinely expressed powers alchemize negativity into a clear seeing of positive possibilities. We get rewired. Actually, we get a new, sleek, reliable operating system.

Whidbey Island is the most amazing place. Across Puget Sound and 30 miles north of Seattle, it is a forested wonderland of gigantic pine trees. Things are nurtured into bigness there, including one's thinking. Recently, I attended a yearlong program there titled Conversational Leadership. It was an arduous journey traveling three times during the year from San Diego to Seattle and then up the coast to catch a ferry over to Whidbey. The chilly ride offered a gradually clear and expansive view of the Whidbey coastline. The retreat center lives in a secluded hollow amidst the massive oaks and pines. Out on a walk one afternoon, the green giants seemed to be talking to me: "Here, in this place where we pine trees pierce the sky and the land is a rain magnet, intensity is in the air you breathe. Let reflection and deep questions insert themselves into your life. Here, you find what stirs your being. Don't come if you don't want to find out." Yes, because I will become responsible for what I know—we all are. Integrity becomes essential to our peace. You might ponder for a moment what deep questions call you to explore a particular power because your happiness and progress want the answers.

DENY AND AFFIRM

- *I release any fear of change and put my trust in the power of Spirit within me.*

- *I surrender my fear into the alchemy of divine love and move forward with courage.*

- *I let go of worry and know that Spirit in me makes straight my way to the good that awaits me.*

PRAY

I open my heart and whole being to the enlightening, energizing presence of Spirit within me. I am empowered to live a resilient life. I am resourced to be magnetic to bountiful blessings today and always. I rest my mind in gratitude for all the good that has been, is now, and all that awaits me today.

PRACTICE

1. Listen to your life. What is it asking of you? Trying to teach you?

2. Know the Truth. Know spiritual principles and how to apply them in life circumstances.

3. Prune what isn't the Truth from your belief system.

4. Visualize the best and let go of the rest.

5. Accumulate good by doing it.

Chapter 5
A 12 Powers Overview

I n the chapters ahead, you will encounter the 12 powers in greater detail. You'll be invited to meditate on each of them. Recognizing that heaven is a state of consciousness, I think of the powers as a map of heaven. In your meditation time, picture the color of each power in its location in your body as dazzling light that fills your every cell and atom, blessing, purifying, and enlivening your body.

Below is a framework to help you visualize these divine powers at work in you, with brief descriptions that will be explored in subsequent chapters.

Power	Disciple	Body	Color
Faith	Peter	Middle Head	Royal Blue
Understanding	Thomas	Mid-Upper Head	Gold
Will	Matthew	Mid-Upper Head	Silver
Imagination	Bartholomew	Third Eye	Light Blue
Power	Philip	Throat	Purple
Zeal	Simon	Nape of Neck	Orange
Love	John	Heart	Pink
Wisdom	James	Solar Plexus	Yellow
Order	James the Lesser	Abdomen	Deep Green
Strength	Andrew	Small of Back	Light Green
Release	Thaddeus	Tailbone	Amber
Life	Judas	Reproductive Organs	Red

FAITH is the foundation of all that we think, say, and do in any given moment. The challenge and shift can occur when we notice what we are putting our faith in by monitoring exactly what we are thinking, saying, and doing.

Jesus often said, "Your faith has made you well." Faith is an internal power that, while invisible, creates our reality—for better or for worse. As a spiritual power, its seed resides in the area of the pituitary gland. This is perfect because the pituitary is the master gland that contributes to physical development, reproduction, vitality, and energy levels. Spiritual faith is the ground of our creative expression, vitality, optimism, and spiritual development.

The powers of **UNDERSTANDING** and **WILL** are located in our frontal lobe. The work of this part of our brain is thinking, planning, problem-solving, emotional and behavioral control—a perfect fit for these two powers that shift mistaken understanding and unreliable self-will into their life-enhancing spiritual expression. For example, surrendering what I want—my self-will—and asking for God's will was scary in the beginning. I first had to believe, through trial and error, that God's will for me is always for an increase of good. Even with lots of practice, it hasn't always been easy. I can be pretty attached to what I want. In the end, it's always been a better idea to just surrender.

The energy of **IMAGINATION** encourages us with beautiful, inspiring pictures of possibilities while supporting the functions of the pineal and pituitary glands along with faith.

POWER transforms energy from one plane of existence to another. How perfect that it abides in the throat where our thoughts become words. Power moves our other powers into action.

The creative energy of **ZEAL** is located in the occipital lobe, which governs our vision. The function of zeal is to move us out of stuck conditions of the mind and life. It responds to what is important to us. Spiritualized zeal inspires us to take action to fulfill our full potential and maximize our gifts so that not only are we happy, joyous, and free, but we make our contribution to life and to supporting the creation of heaven on earth—a world that works for all.

LOVE is at the heart center and, like our physical heart, pumps life, vitality, and vigor throughout our being. This love flows into all areas of our lives, giving us physical, mental, emotional, and spiritual health.

WISDOM is located at the juncture of the stomach and intestines. Like the body-intelligence that sorts out what is physically nourishing to the body from what isn't, spiritual wisdom sorts through our knowledge and marries it to spiritual understanding and love. The outcome: We know what to do, and we do it. We know the next right step and are empowered to take it. We are wise.

ORDER rights all upset, chaos, confusion, and difficulty. It fine-tunes our thinking, emotions, attitudes, and perceptions. It is the astonishing synchronicity of a committed, disciplined spiritual life. Divine order expresses as spiritually grounded priorities. Its place in the body is in the heart of the intestines, a muscle that in concert with surrounding organs and systems, allows the absorption of nutrients and the release of waste, sustaining life, health, and vitality in perfect order.

STRENGTH, located at the base of the spine, is our spiritual backbone, empowering perseverance, courage, and character. While our physical spine supports our body and protects our spinal cord, which is the communication center between our brain and body, the spiritual spine moves strength from our thoughts (hopes, dreams, and desires) to the powers necessary to right action. It fuels the activity of the other powers.

RELEASE, also called *elimination* or *renunciation*, is our power to say *no*. It releases from consciousness what does not serve us. Located at our tailbone, in the area of our physical elimination system, it unclogs our thinking just as a well-functioning elimination system unclogs our body.

LIFE is the creative force of the universe and is our creative vitality. As our sexual organs function to generate new life, life functions to express vitality and creativity. It infuses our other powers with the energy needed to live a good, even powerfully beautiful and productive, life. Spiritualized life chooses the highest, most rewarding expressions of our creative power.

Part Two

Spiritual Mastery, Step-by-Step

Chapter 6

Faith: The Power of Yes

Now faith is the assurance of things hoped for, the conviction of things not seen.

—Hebrews 11:1 (NRSV)

Build a dream and the dream will build you.—Robert Schuller

R obert Schuller had a big dream, a dream that demanded a bigger faith. His congregation had first outgrown the drive-in theater where they started and then a 500-seat sanctuary. He called on renowned architect Philip Johnson, who designed an extraordinary cathedral of glass to match Schuller's big dream. As Howard Kelley, Schuller's stewardship director, tells the story, Schuller asked Johnson, "How much is this going to cost, Philip?" Johnson responded, "Eighteen million, Robert." Kelley said that Schuller, who was an imposing figure at six foot two, pounded his fist on the table and said, "Philip, I don't have $18 million. I don't have $1 million. Philip, I don't have any money, but that church will be built!" And it was.

Schuller believed with all his heart that this astounding church would be built. He didn't see how in that moment, but he had faith that pierced the cloud of unknowing. His divinely grounded faith found a way and he walked in it, one step at a time. That's how it works—one small step at a time, and our faith grows stronger with each step we take. Fears and doubts diminish with each move toward the good we seek.

I had the privilege of getting to know about a remarkable young man named Gary while I was serving Unity Village Chapel in Missouri. His mom came to make arrangements for a celebration of life service after he died.

Gary had been a badge-earning Boy Scout. He served in the U.S. Armed Forces and earned a Purple Heart for his bravery in combat. When he returned home from serving his country, he found a job in an office in his hometown of Lee's Summit, Missouri.

Everybody loved Gary there. He had a unique way of bringing light, love, and joy to everyone each day. Every morning when he walked through the doors, the ongoing hum was interrupted by his greeting: "Feel the love!" Everyone did. Gary was their morning cup of sunshine.

Not long after he started working at this office, however, the energy changed because Gary wasn't there. There was no morning feel-the-love greeting. Gary had not been feeling well for a while and finally went to the doctor. The news was not good. He was diagnosed with brain cancer. Following the diagnosis, he had brain surgery and then months of treatment.

One day with everyone in the office busy at their desks, suddenly the words burst into the quiet, "Feel the love!" You could hear a roar erupt as everyone in unison yelled, "Gary's here!" They ran from their offices to greet him, arms raised just as he did each time he said, "Feel the love!" The joy rang throughout the building.

Gary died only weeks later, but his greeting never will. He boldly expressed love and joy in the midst of excruciating pain, even when he stood on the brink of death. How? He was powered by a faith that was bigger than his diagnosis. You can be too!

Author and religious scholar Reza Aslan argues that our spiritual practice is typically to attribute our own emotions and personalities to God. He asserts that we have inverted the process. Rather than shaping God in our image, we can master life's energies and circumstances by shaping ourselves in the image and likeness of God. Faith actually flourishes when we exhibit the kind of character qualities that Gary did. We, too, can shape ourselves in the form of faith.

Faith, according to Hebrews 11:1, is "the assurance of things hoped for, the conviction of things not seen." In other words, you'll see it when you believe it. Faith gives us the grit to follow our dreams in the face of obstacles and setbacks. It trumps fear. It is the substance of all creative movement and the constructing power of ideas that result in manifestation. It is the faith that Gary and Robert Schuller tapped into.

Our creative energy is always exercising our power of faith in some way—either in the problem or the solution. We put faith in the gas pump to pump gas, not water. We put faith in our bank to deposit our money into our account, not someone else's account. All our waking hours, we are giving the creative power of faith to something. When you begin to pray in faith and take action as faith guides you, you begin the process of developing it along spiritual lines so that you find yourself living full-out.

It was a brilliant sunny day along the shore of the Sea of Galilee as Jesus rested himself. He had just multiplied a few loaves and fish to feed at least 5,000 people who had followed him, hoping for their own miracle. Jesus no doubt needed a rest after such a formidable manifestation of creative power. He told the disciples to get into the boat moored at the shore and head to the other side of the water while he climbed the hill overlooking the Sea of Galilee to renew himself in prayer.

By evening, the disciples were only halfway across when the sea became so turbulent that they feared they were going to drown. In the midst of their terror, Jesus came walking on the water toward the boat. At first the disciples thought they were seeing a ghost, which only exacerbated their fear. Jesus called to them, saying, essentially, "It's me. Don't be afraid." Peter answered, "Lord, if it is you, command me to come to you on the water" (Matthew 14:28). That's definitely courageous. Peter was willing to get out of the boat, trusting that if it really was Jesus, Peter would be empowered to walk on the water.

The rest of the story is what happens to most of us when we do something courageous. We have a fearful thought that begins, "What if I fail?" followed by some tragic, terrifying "then." Those thoughts invariably beget others and pretty soon we begin to sink into the problem like stepping into quicksand.

Peter actually took a few steps on the water but got distracted. He felt a strong gust of wind, shifted to fear, and, sure enough, began to sink. He took his focus off his desire, put it on the perceived danger, and down he went. However, he had the good sense and enough faith in that moment to call out, "Lord, save me!" (Matthew 14:30) Immediately, Jesus reached out his hand and caught Peter. It's always better not to wait until we're drowning before turning to the power of Spirit within us for guidance and help. That is the work of faith.

Jesus asked, "You of little faith, why did you doubt?" (Matthew 14:31) Apparently, Peter didn't have a good answer. When they were both safely back in the boat, the winds ceased. The winds of fear and turbulent water of doubt in our minds cease—

or at least die down to a quiet whisper—when we activate our power of faith.

This illustrates how our level of spiritually developed faith works or it doesn't work.

Faith believes before it sees and feels ahead of time. It can hold you steady in the midst of change, unfavorable winds, and adverse conditions. The strong winds of unfavorable change die down when we ignite our power of faith in a right direction and right outcome.

I recently attended an evening with Jean Houston, an author and forerunner of the Human Potential Movement. She described the power of faith by saying that, "Faith takes the mustard seed of ourselves, replants it in the soil of possibility … and weaves new connections in the brain. It enhances and gives flexibility and color to our motor and sensory capacities, raises our frequency and capacity of thought, evolves the self, and finally grows God in us." Jesus claimed that faith, represented by Peter, is the foundation on which to build a life, a spiritually enriched life.

In Lewis Carroll's *Through the Looking-Glass and What Alice Found There*, Alice finds herself in a strange land and begins to feel lonely and scared. As she dwells on those thoughts, the fear intensifies and she begins to cry. Suddenly the White Queen appears, saying that Alice need not cry and feel sorry for herself. "Consider what a great girl you are. Consider what a long way you've come today. Consider what o-'clock it is. Consider anything, only don't cry!"

In other words, shift your focus to something positive. That's a good start.

In the story, the White Queen shocks Alice then by asserting that she is 101 years, 5 months, and 1 day old. Of course, Alice says, "I can't believe *that*! … One *can't* believe impossible things."

The Queen replies, "I daresay you haven't had much practice ... When I was your age, I always did it for half-an-hour a day. Why, sometimes I've believed as many as six impossible things before breakfast."

Now *that* is a robustly developed resilience born of tested faith. It's a good practice before breakfast, after breakfast, or any time of the day or night!

Still, we all have heart's desires that seem impossible because of internal, self-limiting conversations. Apparently, the White Queen practiced ridding herself of those by mastering her focus. That's the way for us to develop the kind of faith that moves the mountains in our lives. It happens in our minds first. We believe it first, hold our focus steady, and *then* we see it.

At the 2016 National Memorial Day Concert, actor Gary Sinise spoke for a man who lost his leg while serving in Vietnam. The young man, John J. Farley III, wanted to give up on himself and life. It seemed no one wanted to listen to what it was like for him. However, a light was kindled in him, the light of faith, when another veteran came to visit him and actually listened. Farley's faith grew as he held his focus on his almost-forsaken dream. With each step forward, his faith was intensely ignited until the dream of being an attorney came true. He then went on to become a federal judge who helped veterans move through red tape and delays in getting the help they needed.

A mustard seed of faith moves mountains, just as it did for that young man. We all have mountains of sorts in our lives. With mustard seeds of faith, nurtured through small actions, our resilience will flourish so mountains do not stop us.

Thomas Merton, the Christian monk and mystic, wrote in *New Seeds of Contemplation*:

God utters me like a word containing a partial thought of Himself.

A word will never be able to comprehend the voice that utters it.

But if I am true to the concept that God utters in me, if I am true to the thought of [God] I was meant to embody, I shall be full of His actuality and find [God] everywhere in myself ... I shall find myself.

God utters you as a unique-in-all-the-world thought of divine mind, imbued with all that it takes to express that thought, maturing into extraordinary fullness with each faithful (bold, daring, and courageous) step.

Without faith in something greater than our humanness, faith in a power that is within us and all around us, our fears can drive our decisions unconsciously. Without divine faith, hope and optimism wobble. Spirituality is caring well for the life force that is seeking to express as a creative, abundant, vital, and joyful you. Our indwelling spirit seeks to mature just as we do.

I remember chomping at the bit to get my driver's license. Then I could hardly wait to graduate from high school and go off to college. Then I could hardly wait to get a teaching job, then get married. In retrospect, I can see how our spirit incessantly nudges us to grow. It always seems to involve overcoming some fear, much to my chagrin.

My brother Jimmy and his buddy Tommy, feeling a wanderlust and, frankly, not ready to settle down after finishing college, headed to Australia. While Tommy stayed a little less than a year, my brother and another friend decided to travel the world. They traveled by motorcycle, bartering their way from country to country. One February day, my parents received a wire from Indonesia saying that my brother had been involved in a hit-and-run motorcycle accident and was paralyzed. They did not expect him to walk again. My parents refused to believe it. My sisters and I would not, could not, believe it either. Nor, as it turned out, would Jimmy.

We all began a prayer vigil, visualizing him whole and well and walking. My father, practicing his faith, went to his congressman to appeal for help in getting Jimmy home. He was unstoppable in his efforts. Four months later, after my father moved heaven and earth to get my brother back home to Tampa and treated by the best medical team he could find, the miracle happened.

Not knowing what I would find, I flew to Tampa to visit my parents, who were caring for Jimmy. As I walked from the plane and into the terminal at Tampa International Airport, I saw my father and my brother Jimmy walking toward me. There he was, walking, with only a slight limp! Prayers of faith and faithful action can and do generate miracles.

Pope John XXIII said, "Consult not your fears but your hopes and your dreams. Think not about your frustrations, but about your unfulfilled potential. Concern yourself not with what you tried and failed in, but with what is still possible for you to do." Jimmy and my dad would attest to that!

For as long as I can remember in my adult life, I wanted to live on the water. Being near water always energizes me and in some way arouses my creative thinking. When my children were young, we lived in a quiet neighborhood in Chicago, far from Lake Michigan and any body of water. But I dreamed. My husband and I divorced before my son and daughter were in school, and I began to think about moving to a place where being a single mother wasn't the oddity it was in our suburb.

One day I was driving in the area of the school where I had just been hired as a Spanish teacher. Driving around the neighborhoods near Elk Grove High School, I came upon a condominium complex that was built around two beautiful, man-made lakes. Weeping willow trees surrounded one of the lakes and expanses of green grass with winding walking paths surrounded the other.

I called the office the next day and rushed over to meet with the manager. I asked whether there might be an opportunity to rent a unit. He promised he would keep his ears open and let me know. I honestly felt in my heart that it was going to work out. Not more than a month later, he called me to say a unit had become available for one year only. That was enough for me. I jumped at the chance. Before the year was up one of my neighbor's units came on the market. It was on the third floor overlooking the lake with all the willow trees. I put in my offer, and my little ones and I moved in just as my lease on the other unit ended. Passion is a great igniter of faith. The energy of passion-fueled faith opened the way to my dream home. It will for you too.

The disciple Peter represents the power of faith. In you, it is the energy of clear direction, which is fueled by an unshakable faith in a God that is all Good all the time, everywhere present, and the Source of creative energy. In you, it is at once a gift, a skill, and a way of interpreting your experiences. As Jesus said, it is the foundation (rock) on which to build a spiritual life.

Sometime after his attempt to walk on water, Peter had another crisis in faith and, in his fear, he betrayed Jesus. But almost immediately he saw it for what it was—fear, not faith. Most of us know about betraying our best self, the divine spark, when we are afraid. As we grow in practiced faith, we recognize it more quickly, just as Peter did.

Over and over, Jesus assured his followers that their faith in the God within them and all around them could and would move the mountains of fear and struggle in their lives. We develop faith just as we would in training for a marathon, learning to play a musical instrument, or mastering a foreign language. We practice even when it takes effort, even when it strains our believing muscles, and even when it's hard.

When I was living in San Francisco, my friend Neal invited me to join him on Saturday mornings at the dojo that George Leonard founded in Mill Valley, California. It turned out that George, along with the cofounder of Esalen, Michael Murphy, created a practice called ITP—Integral Transformative Practice. It involved meditation, Tai Chi-like movement, and silently affirming three powerful truth statements we each created for ourselves. Each week we shared our experience and progress in a small group. I began to notice something quite amazing. One of my affirmations was, *My capacity to give and receive love increases dramatically. I radiate love and magnetize love.* I loved saying it. It energized me and seemed to deepen my faith that I was actually lovable, rather than fearing that maybe I wasn't. At the time, I so wanted my capacity to love to increase. In retrospect, I see it was a yearning. I wanted love to be an ongoing, in-the-moment experience. I affirmed it daily, first thing in the morning during my prayer time.

Throughout the years, I surprised myself, noticing that I was, in fact, expressing love more freely. This new freedom brought the realization that our capacity to love linked with faith is infinite. It could increase without end—infinitely. That actually felt more empowering. My new affirmation became, *My capacity to give and receive love is infinite. I radiate love and magnetize love.* My faith grew with my practice of those affirmations. Create some affirmations that give you positive energy, and your faith will grow too.

Renowned basketball coach Jim Valvano knew the dojo of life and faith well. Diagnosed with terminal cancer in his forties, he lived there daily the last year and a half of his life.

I recently watched a YouTube video of the speech he gave on March 4, 1993, as he accepted the inaugural Arthur Ashe Courage and Humanitarian Award for his now off-the-court, extraordinarily positive attitude and zest for life. That night, as he walked haltingly and with help up the stairs to the stage, the auditorium erupted in shouts, whistles, and thunderous applause. Tears streamed down the faces of burly athletes, touched by the courage and legacy of this man, by his passion, enthusiasm, and commitment to give his best, while bringing out the best in people throughout his career and even then with his body full of cancer tumors. He gave his acceptance speech with the same great passion and enthusiasm he had always demonstrated.

He said, "When people say to me, 'How do you get through life or each day?' it's the same thing. To me, there are three things we all should do every day ... Number one is laugh. You should laugh every day. Number two is think. You should spend some time in thought. Number three is you should have your emotions moved to tears, could be happiness or joy."

He went on to say, "I urge all of you ... to enjoy your life, the precious moments you have ... To be enthusiastic every day, and ... to keep your dreams alive in spite of problems, whatever you have."

His final words that evening testified to his faith: "What I would like to be able to do is spend whatever time I have left and to give ... some hope to others."

In partnership with ESPN, he established the V Foundation for Cancer Research. Valvano passed away about two months after that speech at a young 47, but his words and the legacy of a passionate, courageous life live on. As you reflect for a moment, what legacy would you like to leave? Your faith in action will accomplish it.

In *The Revealing Word*, Charles Fillmore defined *faith* as "the perceiving power of the mind linked with the power to shape substance ... It is a magnetic power that draws unto us our heart's desire from the invisible spiritual substance." If our faith is significant, our life becomes significant, people are blessed by our presence, and the world becomes a better place because we have walked there.

AFFIRM FAITH

- *I am divine faith expressing. I am confident and expectant of good.*

- *I put feet on my faith, and my faith opens doors to greater good.*

- *My faith is my wand, and I infuse my dreams with it.*

VISUALIZE FAITH

(You might consider recording this visualization and those in the following chapters so you can listen to them with your eyes closed.)

Close your eyes and bring your attention to the center of your head. Begin to breathe into this area, near the pituitary gland, called the master gland, and the hypothalamus that produces endorphins. Imagine with your inner vision a tiny, royal blue light in that area, the color vibration of faith. See it glowing brightly.

As you focus your attention on this royal blue light, notice it growing brighter and shimmering as it expands to fill your whole body. Breathe this brilliant blue light into every cell and atom of your being. Rest and breathe, knowing that divine faith is at work. It knows what to do and is doing it. Little by little, with your willingness and attention, it will dissolve everything unlike itself.

Imagine your deepest desires and fondest dreams infused with the royal blue light of divine faith. Your faith is a laser beaming into the infinite resources of divine substance, drawing your desires and dreams into form. Give thanks. Then in the days ahead, pay attention to clues that will guide you to next right steps.

PRAY FAITH

Most amazing God, thank you for the courage to grow my faith through following my dreams. Thank you for the faith to believe in your divine plan for my life even when I don't see it. Thank you for the courage to put my faith into action in ways that bless me and make me a blessing to others. Thank you for growing in me a brave heart, a high vision, enduring hope, and a taste for all that is good and worthwhile.

PRACTICE FAITH

1. In your prayer time, ask the divine presence in you what your next right steps are. Listen carefully and journal what comes to you. Then do it.

2. Find a prayer partner to help fan your hopes and encourage you. Be that for someone else.

3. Take a small, courageous step each day this week in the direction of one of your heart's desires.

REFLECT ON FAITH

1. If you had enough faith, what would you do?

2. If you had a shade more courage, what would you dare?

3. What might you do to develop robust courage at this time in your life?

4. What conversation with yourself and/or others do you need to stop having to make room for what is trying to emerge in your life?

5. What small step could you take to nurture your divine
   faith?

Chapter 7
Strength: Spiritual Backbone

Fire is the test of gold; adversity, of strong men.—Seneca, *De Providentia*

I love the man that can smile in trouble, that can gather strength from distress, and grow brave by reflection.

—Thomas Paine, *The American Crisis I*

Strength is freedom from weakness, stability of character, power to withstand temptation. It is the force or power to do, capacity to accomplish.

—Charles Fillmore, *Keep a True Lent*

Some years ago, the movie *Braveheart* was breaking records at the box office. The hero, William Wallace, was on an odyssey to avenge his wife's murder. At the beginning of his journey, his heart burned with passion for revenge, but somewhere along the way he experienced a shift. The more he was tested, the more he began to see greatness emerging from the depths of him. He found an incredible strength within himself that transformed his rage for revenge into a commitment to justice and truth. Here in this one man shone a kind of moral and spiritual courage and integrity that made me want to stand and salute and brought tears of recognition—the recognition that lives in you too.

Rigorous strength of soul shone brilliantly and regally in him in the face of darkness. This is the power of spiritual strength, and it's in every one of us. It sustained Wallace in his direction despite the heartbreak and difficulties he encountered. And it will sustain you in your direction too.

Our spiritual odyssey, like those of epic heroes, calls us to uncover and grow the power of strength so that we accomplish our dreams and heart's desires, as we discover who we really are. We dare to pierce the shadows of our current awareness in search of the Holy Grail, the pearl of great price. Jesus called it the kingdom of heaven. It is the divine presence living as strength in us. In the Arthurian legend, Sir Galahad was one of the 12 knights of King Arthur's Knights of the Round Table. His quest for the Holy Grail wasn't really about finding the Grail. It was about Galahad finding his true strength and his true self. His adventures revealed an unquenchable resilience.

I thought it would never return. I sent it into hiding so long ago—my true voice. I sent it into hiding because of an incident that broke my spirit and my heart.

It happened one afternoon at home on Paulina Street in Chicago. I must have been almost 4 years old, but I remember as if it were yesterday. Funny how unhappy memories don't permanently disappear. My mom was rocking my younger sister—2 1/2 years younger to be exact—in our old, wooden rocking chair. I must have been feeling left out, so I came and stood next to them. I had just put my hand on the left arm of the chair when my mom shooed me away. I don't know whether I cried at the time. I do remember backing away and walking to my bedroom, even then numbing myself to the pain. In retrospect, I think my heart constructed a wall around itself, and my true voice got locked in behind it.

Other events strengthened that wall as it became a fortress throughout time. There was the time my mom told me I was too timid; the time in second grade when a nun hit a boy and I started crying. The nun reported this to the principal, who called my parents. How did my mom handle it? She told me that evening that I was too sensitive and had to learn to be stronger. I was not convinced. In fact, my mom's comment ignited embers of fear. I didn't think I could find a way out. I reached out to the God of my little-girl understanding, hoping for a miracle. "Make me strong. Make me strong," I prayed.

Spiritual strength is a power that can trump fear and empower you to take right action in the face of fear, loss, anger, rejection, disappointment, delay, and disapproval. It partners with faith to sustain us on our odyssey to discover and live from the kingdom of heaven within us. It grows with our intentional spiritual development. It rises from noble values and ideals and a passion for what is possible. It is a spiritual muscle and more. It is our spiritual backbone.

Despite my mother's admonition to be strong, a free-floating fear lurked in the shadows, ready to stop me from following my heart or even knowing for sure what I wanted. God forbid I should ask for what I want or need. Forget about sharing my opinion. I distinctly remember the first time someone asked me how I felt. I couldn't answer. I didn't know. Frozen! I had gone numb to myself and was almost totally at the mercy of my fears and others' opinions and needs.

When I was 16, I caught a glimpse of how my fears stopped me from having any sense of belonging in the world, let alone doing what I yearned to do. I was sick and tired of being sick and tired, hiding away in the loneliness of being dominated by fear. I felt like the walking dead. I began to pray, asking God to give me the strength to change and do things differently. The first thing I noticed was a desire for leadership. That was totally unlike anything I had ever thought. Fading into the background seemed far safer.

Yet I began to feel a burning desire to step out from behind myself. I didn't quite know how, but I was willing. Willingness apparently was important. I was elected to class office that year and then, lo and behold, I was invited to be editor of the school newspaper. I was astounded and afraid. At the same time, I was filled with joy that my prayer seemed to be answered. I felt strong, perhaps for the first time in my life. Walking from school to the bus stop that day, I heard for the first time a clear, strong voice in me say, *No more regrets. I will not live with regrets.*

Years later, my friend Ken lost sight of his dreams amid the negativity and challenge of his workplace. Tending to complaints and the constant pressure from people who wanted him to execute their "good ideas" wore him down. He felt a sense of inadequacy and discouragement. Finding other job opportunities began to look very attractive. He began to fantasize about greener pastures in the face of feeling unappreciated and unable to meet the demands of his job.

In an effort to encourage him, I told him the story about my friend Mark. Fortune seemed to smile on Mark and his wife Cindy when his employer offered him a great opportunity to transfer from the cold Kansas City metro area to sunny San Diego, California, as head of operations at the company's manufacturing plant there. As hard as it was for them to leave the comfort of familiar people and places in Kansas City, the chance to live in San Diego and the promotion proved irresistible.

It didn't take long for Mark to endear himself to the people who worked for him. He loved his job and their new life in Southern California. Imagine how shocked he was, then, when told in his performance evaluation that he didn't measure up. It took all of the strength he could muster to find his brave heart again. He wanted to quit on the spot and find other opportunities. But he didn't. Instead, he prayed for the strength to stay. His prayer and pure motive ignited a remarkable kind of strength in him. He made a decision to give his best each day and to continue to support and encourage his people to do the same.

Shortly after that, he was told that Corporate decided to shut down his manufacturing plant, and it was his job to tell the employees their jobs would be eliminated within the next six months. Mark got with himself and his God again to seek guidance. The following day he gathered his employees together to make the announcement. He told them how proud he was of them and how grateful he was to work with them. Then he challenged them just as he had challenged himself. "Let's go out on top," he said. "Let's give our best and show how great we are."

When the statistics came out at the end of the year, Mark's plant and his team were not only the top producers but led the country in job satisfaction within the corporation. This, even in the midst of knowing none of them would have a job soon. Because of Mark's strength of character, they all went out on top.

Helen Keller said, "Faith is the strength by which a shattered world shall emerge into the light." After having their world shattered, Mark and his employees emerged into the light of radiant strength.

Spiritual strength informs all of our other spiritual capacities. It bridges faith to action. It musters compassion for our own and others' human shortcomings and difficulties. At the same time, we are empowered to rise above any difficulty or personal upset to do the most loving, effective thing. It is the power to tell the truth when it might cost us. It is the power to acknowledge a mistake or fault rather than make an excuse, defend, or justify.

It is the power to go the extra mile even when we are physically, mentally, or emotionally exhausted.

Sheryl Sandberg, COO of Facebook, wrote in her book *Option B: Facing Adversity, Building Resilience, and Finding Joy* (Knopf, 2017) of the devastation she experienced with the shocking death of her husband David, the love of her life. She couldn't find her own resilience. In fact, for a while she wasn't even looking for it. As the days passed, she realized that she needed to take action to access her resilience and move forward in her life. She began to take little steps. She became willing to be vulnerable and shared her deepest feelings with a dear friend. She decided to write about it and, in the process, discovered a new kind of resilience. She came to realize that her experience could benefit others. She made that her heartfelt desire and, in that, became a radiant light of hope for others.

Spiritualized strength is the power to stand in the spiritual truth we know, to practice spiritual principles even when it is difficult, and to act courageously with authentic spiritual motives. This strength supports the activity of empowered and sustained direction.

It was an overcast November day when I met my friend Eileen at 6:30 a.m. at Denny's. As we headed for Balboa Park to set up for Team Jenn, the sun began to break through the clouds. The reason for our drive at such an ungodly hour was to participate in a five-mile Save A Life Walk.

Eileen, along with other parents and loved ones, had created walking teams to honor those who had taken their own lives. Eileen's daughter Jennifer had taken her life at age 42. She had battled drug addiction for years and ended her struggle one weekend while alone in her apartment. At the end of our walk, we stood together as a bugler played "Taps." Eileen released a dove, confident that Jenn's spirit had taken flight into a mysterious dimension most of us only guess at.

Eileen had gathered the strength to create a team of her friends who wanted to support her by walking with her that day. Her faith had gone into crisis when notified of Jennifer's suicide, but it did not die. The inherent divine spark in her grew into an enormous flame as she sought and found a way to heal her heart and honor her beautiful daughter.

The Roman philosopher and statesman Seneca is quoted as saying in his *Moral Letters*, "It is not because things are difficult that we do not dare. It is because we do not dare that things are difficult." Eileen would agree. She used her strength to step out of her grief and guilt and dare something for the sake of love.

Having heroes and heroines is important. They inspire our strength by demonstrating their own. Take Jesus. He showed remarkable strength in the face of insult, disappointment, loss, betrayal, public humiliation, and excruciating torture. He had his moments, just like all of us. He even had a crisis in faith, feeling forsaken by God. That crisis, however, did not turn him to bitterness and despair. He surrendered into it. He dug deep into his reservoir of faith and strength and came out of the tragic ordeal in stunning radiance.

Thank God we have heroes and heroines who inspire us to be more than our circumstances, who inspire us to overcome our difficulties. My troubles seem to dissolve when I see or read about those who have risen out of the darkness of wounds to body and/ or soul—Gandhi, Martin Luther King Jr., Mother Teresa, Jim Valvano, Helen Keller—and all of our soldiers who have been harmed in service to their country, but nevertheless have risen to create a new life.

The regular trips to Whidbey Island I mentioned earlier were motivated by the allure of a kind of leadership dojo initiated by poet David Whyte. The goal of his Conversational Leadership program was for us to discover our own artistry in the world and courageously bring it to bear not only in our workplaces but in all our relationships. Part of our assignment included choosing an artist to study. Who inspires us in our own lives? Whose artistry in the world encourages our own?

I chose Andrea Bocelli, blind from the age of 12. While his breathtaking tenor voice sends chills up my spine, I chose him for the astounding things he has accomplished despite not having sight. He rides horses bareback, skateboards, and plays multiple instruments.

He said something once in an interview that touched on the fact that, like all of our gifts, strength develops through valuing your gift and developing it. He said he had to invest himself completely in doing this. He lives passionately, expanding the borders of his blindness in unprecedented ways. Our heroes and heroines are essential in that way. They inspire us to grow our gifts through the power of our inherent gift of strength. The more we grow our strength by walking through our fears, the more we grow a bigger conception of God and a bigger life.

In the film *The Curious Case of Benjamin Button*, Button says, "For what it's worth: It's never too late ... to be whoever you want to be ... I hope you live a life you're proud of. And if you find that you're not, I hope you have the strength to start all over again." It's never too late! Spiritual strength is our spiritual backbone that empowers us to do what our humanness alone might not.

AFFIRM STRENGTH

- *The strength of God in me gives me all the power I need to lead the life I dream of.*

- *I act on the Truth I know, the values I hold dear, and the desires of my heart.*

- *The more I exercise my faith in the divine presence in me, the stronger I become to do even greater things.*

VISUALIZE STRENGTH

Gently close your eyes; breathe deeply, drawing your breath down your backbone. In your mind's eye, see the light-green light of divine strength illuminate the small of your back and begin to pulse up and down your spine. Breathe the shimmering pale green light of divine strength throughout your body. See the pulsating, spiraling green fill your whole being with life-giving spiritual strength. As you breathe the sparkling green light of strength throughout your being, notice your mind clearing and your deepest desires coming into focus. Your noblest and most exciting intentions become clearer. Your next right steps are revealed. Right action becomes irresistible. You feel an expanding sense of effervescent hope. You know what to do and have the power to do it. See yourself living in the answer to your prayers.

PRAY STRENGTH

Spirit of strength, I open myself and my whole life to your power. I give thanks that your strength now builds me into the person you want me to be. Strengthened by your power in me, obstacles become opportunities and I take action that overcomes them. I am grateful for the new clarity and firm purpose. I go forward confidently.

PRACTICE STRENGTH

1. Is there a conversation you need to have that you have been putting off? If so, pray for the strength to speak your truth in love.

2. Wear light green—a scarf, jewelry, article of clothing—as an affirmation that God within is strengthening you to do what God is calling you to do, what matters most, and what makes your heart happy.

3. Create an affirmation that energizes you. You might begin it with *"God in me now strengthens me to ..."*

REFLECT ON STRENGTH

1. What in your life do you want spiritual strength for?

2. What is the most important conversation that you need to stop having with yourself?

3. What is the most important, and maybe the most difficult, conversation that you need to have with another person in your life that perhaps you have been putting off?

Chapter 8

Understanding: Know Beyond What You See

Happy is the man who finds wisdom, and the man who gets understanding, for the gain from it is better than gain from silver and its profit better than gold.

—Proverbs 3:13-14 (RSV)

Divine understanding is the perceiving power of the mind ... Spiritual understanding gives clear insight into everything, it remolds the mentality, and inspires the will to direct, to act, and to control.

—Cora Fillmore, *Christ Enthroned in Man*

Trust in the Lord with all your heart, and do not rely on your own insight. In all your ways acknowledge him, and he will make straight your paths.

—Proverbs 3:5-6 (RSV)

My daughter Jennifer has a friend, Lori, who has always lived on the edge of sane behavior. She and Jennifer have been friends since they were 15 years old. When they were in their twenties, they went on an excursion to Palm Springs. For some reason, Lori got very angry with Jennifer. As Lori's voice rose, Jennifer pulled the convertible over to a parking place. She had no sooner put the car in park when Lori began screaming and summarily jumped out.

Jennifer said later the things Lori screamed at her hurt a lot but, to her amazement, she was able to see beyond Lori's words and behavior. In a moment of grace, Jennifer touched a kind of understanding that gave her the courage to get out of the car and run after her friend. When she caught up to her, she embraced Lori and held her close, telling Lori she loved her. Lori calmed down and, through Jennifer's demonstration of compassionate understanding, was able to find the love in her own heart. Jennifer told me, "I felt so happy because I know that I did the right and loving thing." It was divine understanding expressing, holding two friends together in the arms of love.

True peace of soul is the fruit of spiritual understanding applied to all of the ins and outs, ups and downs, delights and disappointments, successes and failures of life. It can come in a flash of intuitive knowing or through an experience. Just as the disciple Thomas, who represents spiritual understanding, wanted evidence of the power of Spirit in him, we want to see the power of God proved in our lives too.

Paul's prayer for the Ephesians was that their hearts might be enlightened to the truth of the divine power at their command. Spiritual understanding comes with seeking it and with realizing that human understanding alone doesn't always produce good results. We use our spiritual understanding when we make lemonade out of the lemons in life.

King Solomon of the Bible, considered in his day to be one of the wisest and most prosperous of all human beings, asked God for only one thing. Scripture tells us God had offered to give him anything he wanted—anything! If you were given the same offer, what would you ask for?

Solomon, in a moment of solitude and clarity, asked for something intangible. He asked for an "understanding heart" so that he would be empowered to "judge Your people, that I may discern between good and evil" (1 Kings 3:9 NKJV).

Spiritualized understanding is a precious jewel that taps into the infinite spring-fed well of compassion. It takes us gently beneath the facts of life—the circumstances, emotions, and perceptions—to a truer seeing. Through the surface of whatever our eyes can see and our minds interpret, spiritual understanding drops a plumb line to universal Truth. This dissolves the crusted edges of the facts into the nourishing nectar of acceptance, forgiveness, humility, and compassion. Our inner vision is infused with the divine perspective through our willingness to see the situation or person differently. Out of this comes a quintessential understanding of right action.

For example, with spiritual understanding we come to see how our experience can benefit others, and out of this comes greater resilience. This is part of the spiritual alchemy of developing your spiritual powers.

There are universal spiritual laws that live and operate whether we are aware of them or not. If our thinking and responding to life are in alignment with these laws, life works. We find that even in the midst of the greatest difficulty, there is an ineffable sense of clarity that leads to beneficial action. Spiritual understanding gives us the vision to see through the mists of our experience to the highest, most life-enhancing Truth. It helps us find the miracle and meaning in the mess. In this awareness, we can make informed decisions about our responses to people and life's circumstances rather than reacting.

In our willingness, spiritualized understanding redeems our losses, failures, heartbreaks, and fears. It helps transform pain to gain because we see it differently. As the beloved Unity minister Rev. Eric Butterworth said in *Discover the Power Within You*, "Man is not in the world to set it right but to see it rightly." Spiritual understanding is the doorway to using our experience to enrich rather than embitter our lives.

How do we spiritualize our understanding? Start by praying to see beyond troubling appearances, situations, and circumstances. Ask to understand the person or situation from a spiritual perspective. Be willing to see it differently. Pray to see the person or situation differently.

Call on the powers of *love* (forgiveness, compassion) and *release* to inform your thinking. You'll read about these powers later. Give thanks for their coming to assist and guide your thinking and actions. Let go of any person or situation troubling you into the alchemy of divine energy—just think about something else. Wear the color of understanding as a reminder—gold. Stay steady in your release until you feel some sense of peace and notice that your perspective has shifted. The affirmations at the end of this chapter may be helpful or you may create your own.

"No one ever attained spiritual consciousness without striving for it," said Charles Fillmore in *The Twelve Powers of Man*. "Make your mind receptive to the higher understanding through silent meditations and affirmations of Truth. The earnest desire to understand spiritual things will open the way and revelations within and without will follow."

White Eagle had followed his dream to the San Francisco Opera. His rich, voluminous tenor voice won him accolades and garnered the attention of Robert Schuller, founder of the Crystal Cathedral near Los Angeles. White Eagle became a regular soloist there. Rev. Jack Boland, a friend of Schuller's, was equally impressed with White Eagle's voice and made him a regular soloist at the Church of Today in Warren, Michigan. One Sunday morning at the Church of Today, having smelled alcohol on White Eagle's breath more than once, Boland confronted him about his drinking. Jack understood the disease well and knew another alcoholic when he saw one. Because he understood, he could look past the appearance of this man who came to church inebriated. He spoke with compassion and clarity, telling White Eagle that unless he did something about his drinking, he would not be singing at the Church of Today again. White Eagle's heart and understanding broke open. He surrendered into the truth about himself. He actually did do something about his drinking—he quit, thanks to having his spiritual understanding awakened by another.

Divine understanding can generate the ability to see through circumstances to the Truth at the core. It may not come in a moment or as fast as we'd like, at least it didn't for me. But just practicing the foundational truth that I heard early on—change your mind, change your life—hooked me. I wanted to know more. What I found is that the more spiritual truth I came to believe, the more empowered my spiritual understanding became. I didn't keep repeating the same mistakes, thinking I'd get a different result. I was less likely to live in the fight-or-flight syndrome in relationships. Divine understanding will guide you, too, to look for a solution rather than focus on the problem.

As Solomon prayed for an understanding heart, so can we. Step-by-step, its manifestation will create healthy, harmonious relationships along with seeing the circumstances of our lives in the most helpful, life-enhancing, peace-producing way.

After my mom died, my dad was more than ready to follow her. He adored her and when she was gone, he just didn't have much interest in living. He would drive himself to Clearwater Beach each day for weeks and send his love on waves of thought to her. In his profound grief, he rushed into selling the home he and my mom loved so much. Their home rested on the Intracoastal Waterway facing west toward the Gulf of Mexico.

They had spent many happy evenings on their lanai enjoying the sunsets. Dad sold this haven of joy-turned-to-sadness for a drab, second-floor condominium just blocks away. He began to decline quickly. His immense grief was taking its toll. My brother and sister-in-law saw the writing on the wall and built a little studio apartment for him adjacent to their home in Houston. One day, finding him alone in his living room as if in a daze, I called my brother, Jimmy, and told him it was time to bring dad to Houston to live with them.

Jimmy flew into Clearwater with a ticket to take dad back with him. My dad didn't want to go. He didn't want to leave my mom, whose ashes were in a mausoleum in Clearwater. I don't know what my brother said to convince him to get on the plane, but he finally did. Once at my brother's home, it was as if my dad could finally let go of steeling himself through the years of caring for my mom and the grief of losing her. Still, his undiagnosed colon cancer was decimating his body. My brother shared how he would get angry with my dad for not taking his medicine and not eating. As Jimmy tells it, "Dad would touch my hand and tell me not to worry. He'd thank me for taking good care of him." My dad, a former FBI-trained, crusty police captain, had melted into an understanding heart. Sometimes it takes a heartbreaking loss to release the immense beauty and power of divine understanding.

Divine understanding preserves us from living with regrets by revealing better choices than our fragile human understanding would choose. It takes us out of the blame game into asking, "What can I learn?" or "What is Spirit trying to tell me?"

Take St. Benedict's Prep in Newark, New Jersey. The red brick school has defied statistics year after year since the 1970s when a 26-year-old man with a vision took the helm and brought back to life what had seemed dead. His understanding faith pierced through the circumstances of urban blight, riots, a culture of violence, drugs, and hopelessness. Father Edwin Leahy, O.S.B., who had been educated at St. Benedict's himself and lived in the adjacent monastery, resurrected both school and monastery. He understood the human heart and soul. He believed in the greatness within each person and created a school environment that summons greatness from 700-plus students, who probably would never otherwise believe in any greatness within themselves.

St. Benedict's statistics are impressive. According to the school, 98 percent of its graduates go on to college, and 87 percent graduate from college or remain enrolled. Contrast that to the 12 percent of the Newark adult population with a college degree, less than half the national average. Every morning the boys gather in the gym to start their day with a sort of pep rally. Each boy says "I love you, brother" to the boy sitting next to him. They go off to their first class shouting together, "You can be anything you want to be. Go out and conquer." They enlighten the eyes of each other's hearts just as the apostle Paul did with the Ephesians.

Paul wrote to the Ephesians urging, "With the eyes of your heart enlightened, you may [understand] what is the hope to which he has called you, what are the riches of his glorious inheritance" (Ephesians 1:18). In other words, may we come to understand that we have the immense riches of the creative power of God in us to create a life that we love and that contributes to others. Father Edwin Leahy empowers his students to understand and apply this truth. Father Leahy is a spiritual alchemist—and so are you!

One of the classes I love to facilitate is "Mastering Life's Energies," based on a book by my friend Maria Nemeth. Just saying those three words energizes me. Jesus could have written the material. Instead, he talked, taught, and lived it. It's simple—change your mind, change your life. Change what you focus on, change your experience. We can master our thinking and emotions, or they master us and drive our behavior—often without our realizing it. It may sound easy but is incredibly rigorous.

How can we check ourselves? We can ask: Am I giving my creative energy to what really matters to me? Am I mastering what I do with my creative energy—my thoughts, emotions, vitality; in my relationships, work, finances? Am I doing my best to be my best, even when it takes everything I've got, even when an unhelpful reaction is right on the tip of my tongue, even when it would be so satisfying to match someone else's bad behavior—satisfying only for a moment, however? It's about understanding that we have been given the biggest freedom of all—the freedom of choice.

Jesus' life demonstrated his mastery of life's energies, and his teachings show us how to do it too. He didn't spend time analyzing problems ad infinitum. He didn't retaliate. He didn't match bad behavior. His spiritual understanding empowered him to assess the situation and take action to make things better. With his enlightened understanding, he turned people and situations around. We have the power to do this too.

In scripture, the exemplar of awakened understanding is Thomas. Historically, he is referred to as doubting Thomas. He wanted proof that Jesus had risen. Jesus accommodated his doubts by inviting Thomas to touch his wounds. In a similar way, we also want proof that practicing forgiveness, for example, will bring us peace and will open the doorway to greater freedom.

Synchronically, the location of the spiritual power of understanding is in the frontal lobe of the brain, the center of most of the dopamine-sensitive neurons. The frontal cortex governs actions of all kinds, including speech and emotions. It gives us the ability to project the future consequences of what we are about to say or do. It governs our capacity to suppress unacceptable behavior. Developing our understanding into its spiritual potential leads the way to making best choices and taking right action. Its twin is divine will, which is right next to it up there in the frontal cortex. The color vibration associated with spiritual understanding is gold. It empowers us to turn the ore of our lives into gold.

AFFIRM UNDERSTANDING

- *I give thanks that spiritual understanding now dissolves all misunderstandings in me.*

- *The more I understand spiritual principles, the more I understand myself and others.*

- *I see the positive possibility in the problem, and I act from it.*

VISUALIZE UNDERSTANDING

Close your eyes and take a deep, long, full breath of the golden light of understanding. See it glowing in the area just back of your forehead and breathe the golden light throughout your body from head-to-toe. See it sparkle and shine as it fills every cell and atom. All memories are infused with the gifts of spiritual understanding. All hopes and dreams are now permeated with spiritual understanding that guides your next right steps. Breathe the golden light into the depths of your being, where it heals what needs to be healed and reveals what needs to be revealed so that you may do what needs to be done.

PRAY UNDERSTANDING

Loving Lord, I give thanks that the activity of your presence in me enlightens my heart with spiritual understanding. Thank you for opening the eyes of my heart to see my way through fears and tears, regrets and resentments. When I am afraid, thank you for awakening my understanding to act with courage and confidence.

PRACTICE UNDERSTANDING

1. For the next 21 days, pray for an understanding heart. Notice any changes in your thinking or experiences.

2. Wear gold as a reminder that you are growing in spiritual understanding and will intuitively know how to handle situations that used to baffle you.

3. Consider someone in your life who is difficult to love. Look beyond what makes the person difficult to love and find a reason for their behavior that awakens your compassionate understanding.

REFLECT ON UNDERSTANDING

1. What spiritual truth has been most helpful to you? How?

2. How might you be more understanding with yourself?

3. What would an understanding heart empower you to see more clearly, judge more kindly, right now?

Chapter 9

Power: The Energy of Transformation

Power is increased through exalted ideas ... There is a universal, creative force that urges man forward to the recognition of the creative power of his individual thought.

—Charles Fillmore, *The Revealing Word*

The power center in the throat controls all the vibratory energies of the organism. It is the open door between the formless and the formed worlds.

—Charles Fillmore, *The Twelve Powers of Man*

Sheryl loved her work with the children's ministry. She would create the most amazingly clear object lessons for the kids. One Sunday, she demonstrated the nature of spiritual power by wearing a series of electric power cords around her waist—just picture that! Of course, the children's imaginations and curiosity were triggered. Sheryl explained the idea of power cords by telling the children that each of them possessed limitless creative power. She said, "There are many ways to use your power." She then walked around the room plugging one of the cords here and another there into the electrical outlets. "You can plug your cord of power into being happy or sad, kind or mad. You get to decide. For example, if someone at school calls you a name and you get angry and call them names back, what have you done with your power?" The children understood it—that they get to choose what they do with their limitless creative power.

We have a power cord called *thought*. We can plug our thoughts into any idea we choose. We can give our power away to what others are saying or doing. Sometimes we let circumstances dictate our thoughts, or we can take dominion of our power by mastering what we do with it. There is the "observer self" in us that can and will monitor our thoughts. We can catch ourselves thinking! That being the case, we can pause when anxious or agitated and observe the nature of our thoughts. We can unplug our power cord from the problem and plug it into a spiritual solution.

My friend Stacy was mistaken about where to plug in her power cord. She would attach it to other people and circumstances regularly, and then blame them for her unhappiness. She tried plugging it into her husband. It didn't work at all. Fighting became a pattern in their lives. It grew the "fight" energy in her. It didn't make her happy either. She was making herself a victim without realizing it.

My favorite spiritual teacher Marvin Anderson described it this way: People run around dangling their power cords behind them, plugging them in here and there and everywhere except into the True Source that is within and all around them.

Divine power is the creative energy that fuels the whole system. It is the conduit from invisible to visible. The metaphysical center of power is the throat. Just as the throat gives voice to our thoughts, this power stimulates the 11 other creative energies. For example, power energizes us to put our faith into action. Power kicks divine wisdom into gear to make good decisions and take right action. The disciple Philip is the exemplar of power in this framework. The root of the name is Greek and means "lover of horses." We speak of horsepower in cars and in people. It is energy in action.

When I was 15, I suddenly stopped menstruating. I was puzzled but really okay with it. My mother on the other hand was deeply concerned. She never said it, but I suspected she was afraid I was pregnant. After a number of tests, the doctor determined I had a thyroid dysfunction, meaning my thyroid was dramatically underactive. As years passed, I came to see what a perfect metaphor that was for the creative power of power that is "seated" right next to the thyroid. I had been giving away my power all my life for fear of making a mistake, not being smart enough, and not being liked. I began, unconsciously of course, to practice reading minds and adjusting my behavior to preclude mistakes, to generate a kind of perfectionism, and to be accepted. It didn't work well at all. I had no definite sense of personal power—or any kind of power for that matter.

As early as I can remember, fear seemed to lurk around every corner. In my home, it was too scary to ask for what I wanted, say what I didn't like, or offer a differing opinion. I didn't feel safe. My dad's anger was explosive. My mom was a quiet woman who remained silent in the face of his anger. Safety seemed to require silence. One day I came to see that fear of speaking my needs and desires was more painful than the risk of giving voice to them. It didn't come in a day or a week or even a year. It came from noticing repeated moments of pain and, one little step after another, reclaiming my power by doing what I was afraid to do, to speak up instead of shut down.

Whatever we do out of fear, anger, or resentment is an act of giving our power away. We relinquish living an empowered life for an impoverished life.

I've saved a picture of one of the great architectural feats imagined by architect Santiago Calatrava. The picture in *Time* magazine of his proposed architectural wonder reminded me of a jumbo Dairy Queen swirled vanilla ice cream cone. His design was called the Chicago Spire, a soaring, swirling magnificence. A *Time* magazine profile of the architect says, "Calatrava … accomplishes what only great architects can: he creates transcendent spaces that uplift the human spirit." This is power firing the creative genius of one man's vision in ways that inspire the world. For better or for worse, our power ignites our mind, soul, and body. It all depends on where we plug in our power cord. Grounding it in the Divine, inviting divine ideas—nothing more, nothing less—is key to not only creating our life as a work of art but also putting our artistry to all that we do. Divine power is our unstoppable resilience. It gives voice to our thoughts. What we give voice to vibrates throughout the body. Like our thoughts, our words are nonlocal and generate a response from the universe as well as our internal world. Power is the instrument of creativity that generates forward momentum in every area of our lives.

D.J. Gregory came into this world with immense challenges to his power as well as his life. Born with cerebral palsy, underdeveloped lungs, and his legs entangled, the doctors told his parents he would never walk. Fortunately, his parents didn't put their faith in that. They put their faith in a divine possibility and powered up with positive thinking and wise action to make a way for their baby boy.

D.J. went through five surgeries on his legs before first grade. With his parents' support, he came to believe that he would walk. Little by little, he was able to move from a wheelchair to a walker, then to crutches, and finally a cane. He found a power in himself far greater than all of his doctors' doubts.

He loved sports but couldn't play, that is, until he was introduced to golf at 9 years old. He managed to teach himself a one-handed swing. The other hand steadied him on his cane.

When he turned 12, new power and resolve was ignited in him when his dad took him to his first golf tournament. Energized and inspired, he set a goal that day to walk every hole of every round on the PGA Tour. His dad tried to dissuade him, saying that no one, not even the pros, do that. D.J. stood firm. He practiced and practiced. He set a date—the 2008 PGA Tour. The Tour officials said *yes*, and the rest is astounding. D.J. did it—walking nearly 1,000 miles. He has inspired millions since then as he continues to walk to raise money for challenged kids. He discovered an inexhaustible well of resilience in him, the power of his Creator, his spirit.

In 2018 the world witnessed yet another school massacre that killed 17 students and teachers. A 19-year-old gunman toted an AR-15 rifle to Marjory Stoneman Douglas High School in Parkland, Florida. After entering the school, he opened fire in the hallways as students ran for their lives. The gunman had used his creative power to nurse hatred that turned to violence and destruction.

But the light of resilience went on in Parkland, Florida, in the aftermath of this shooting. A few courageous survivors decided enough was enough. Four teenagers stood up and said no more. They organized and directed the power at their command to take positive action. As a result of their courage to speak out, on March 24, 2018, more than a million students across the country left class in protest of the school-shooting epidemic. Millions of hearts, both student and adult, were deeply touched. They put their outrage to the cause for life. The March for Our Lives has continued, bringing millions to the streets hoping to, at last, change the hearts, minds, and motives of lawmakers. Divinely motivated power is unstoppable.

What our power can create is limitless. Consider this: In May of 2012, Sam Groth's tennis serve clocked in at 163.7 mph. At that speed, you can barely see the ball coming! The most powerful nonexperimental airplane, the USAF SR-71 Blackbird, can travel in excess of Mach 3—three times faster than the speed of sound. And the world's fastest passenger plane was the Concorde at 1,354 mph, more than Mach 2. Are you ready for a real shocker? NASA's X-43A aircraft flew at Mach 9.6 or 7,000 mph!

These mind-blowing statistics invite these reflections: Human beings conceived, believed, and harnessed the invisible power that created the Blackbird, Concorde, and X-43A. Human beings have accessed the kind of power that repeatedly expands the reach and impact of our creative energy. The scientists and engineers harnessed the power that inspired their imaginations to do the seeming impossible. Your power does this too.

There is extraordinary power available beyond what you have yet imagined. It can show up in ways unique to each of us—the power to finish a project, manifest a dream, leave an unhealthy situation, design an extraordinary building, create a new recipe, or fix a broken toy.

Just like all those amazing demonstrations of creative power, divine power in you can ignite all of your capacities to their full potential.

AFFIRM POWER
- *The infinite power of God in me enlightens my mind and arouses my heart, giving me the power to say what needs to be said and do what needs to be done for my highest good.*

- *In stillness, I rest in the power of God, and my creative energy is renewed. I make wise decisions and take enlivening action.*

- *I focus on what I love, and what I love empowers me to do it.*

VISUALIZE POWER

Take a deep head-to-toe breath, and another. In your mind's eye, see a sparkling purple light in your throat. As you breathe, see the shimmering purple light expand to fill your whole being. Linger with this vision, watching the spiraling, brilliant purple light, knowing that it is dissolving doubts, worries, and fears so that your true self shines, guiding you to say what needs to be said and do what needs to be done to bless yourself and others. Affirm that it is bringing the resources of Spirit to energize your mind and body with its radiant, empowering energy. Breathe deep and rest in the power of God in you, energizing you to pursue your fondest hopes and highest dreams.

PRAY POWER

Connecting to your power in me and all around me, most Awesome Spirit, I give thanks for the energy to move forward in my life to all that is enriching, enlivening, and worthy. I give thanks that your divine power, quickened and activated in me now, moves me in positive, productive, and purposeful directions.

PRACTICE POWER

1. For the next week, wear something purple, the color vibration for power.

2. With the intention to develop your divine power, consciously do one good deed each day this week (make a phone call to a friend, write a thank-you card, and so on).

3. Speak up for yourself in a situation in which you feel shy or fearful.

REFLECT ON POWER

1. In what kinds of circumstances are you inclined to give your power away? What might you do the next time instead?

2. What is a situation in which you felt your true power? What did you experience?

3. What are the three most important things for you to do this year to utilize your divine power?

Chapter 10
Love: The Soul of Creativity

We love because he [God] first loved us.—1 John 4:19 (NRSV)

I believe that the meaning of life for each one of us is solely to increase [the] love within us ... I believe that the growth of love will contribute more than any other force to establish on this earth the kingdom of God.

—Leo Tolstoy, *My Reply to the Synod's Edict of Excommunication*

Atalented violinist was scheduled to play before a very critical audience and, though she had a fine violin, she wasn't satisfied with the quality of the sound. She told her father she planned to buy some tested strings so her violin would yield its full resonance and tonal vibration. Her father asked how the strings were tested. She explained that first, they're put on a rack and stretched to take all the unsteadiness out of them. Then they are hammered. Then they are put through a chemical test. This is what enables them to produce a perfect, full tone.

I read that story long ago. Sometimes I've felt as if I were those strings being stretched and hammered in the name of a spiritual kind of love, calling me to forgive what I considered unforgivable; calling me to let go of being so easily hurt and to learn a new way of perceiving and being. The story opened me to see difficult experiences differently—maybe not immediately, but with reflection and prayer. I noticed—and still do—that my capacity to love expanded.

I love the movie *A Beautiful Mind* for its portrayal of unconditional love. Even if it doesn't exactly stick to the facts about John Nash, the renowned mathematician who struggled with paranoid schizophrenia, I am drawn to screenwriter Akiva Goldsman's idea that, in the end, Nash discovered the power of love.

In the movie, Nash, played by Russell Crowe, accepts the 1994 Nobel Prize in Economic Sciences, saying, "I've always believed in numbers and the equations and logics that lead to reason ... My quest has taken me through the physical, the metaphysical, the delusional—and back. I have made the most important discovery of my career, the most important discovery of my life: It is only in the mysterious equations of love that any logical reasons can be found."

One of the mysteries of the power of divine love is that it heals. A dear friend of mine shared that her daughter struggled with voices telling her she was not worthy or deserving of happiness and love. In the movie, John Nash had a name for that voice, Charles. Jesus, too, had a name for that voice. He called it The Adversary.

We all confront thoughts that tell us negative things about ourselves and others, thoughts that inhibit our willingness to love, to give, and to grow. It is an inner voice with many disguises. Under all of them is fear.

Jesus, along with other spiritual masters, suggested forgiving the voice. Part of the reconciliation is to realize it is part of being human. Yet there is a power in us that trumps that voice. It is the power of love. When confronted with that negative voice, we can choose to simply acknowledge its presence and turn our attention to someone or something we love. We can even demonstrate a radical kind of love, and with compassion, treat the voice like a scared child.

Jesus spoke of this radical love, a kind of love that could heal the world and the violence in it. He said, "Love your enemies and pray for those who persecute you" (Matthew 5:44). The truth is that only a divinized love could do this. Our humanness falters in the face of hurt, betrayal, fear, or hate. Our hearts are tender and easily bruised. Yet divine love is a power greater than our own human understanding and capacity to love.

When our capacity to love is up-leveled—through willingness to see differently and act differently, and through practicing prayer and meditation—our consciousness is transformed. This kind of love generates kindness and compassion, tolerance and patience, acceptance and appreciation.

St. Augustine said, "Love and do what you will." That's how powerful spiritually grounded love is. It is goodwill in action. It holds the universe together by its constructive, dynamic, and unifying power. It is a solvent for perceived limitations.

When I had the good fortune to attend a Brian Swimme retreat at Dominican University of California in San Rafael, our exploration was "The Powers of the Universe." He said, "To become aware of these powers is to touch the source of life … Contemplating the wonders of the unfolding creativity of the cosmos is a mystical, ecstatic, awe-inspiring event."

One of those powers (interestingly, 12 of them) he called *allurement*. He described allurement as an attracting power and one that holds things together. This is the power of love. In *Prosperity*, Unity cofounder Charles Fillmore says, "Love is the world's greatest attractive power."

Divine love roots our thoughts, words, and actions in heavenly soil. Our character takes on an elegant beauty that warms and welcomes. We have the capacity to build people up rather than tear them down, to concern ourselves with what we can contribute rather than what we can get. A wintry frame of mind becomes a fragrant summertime frame of mind.

In one of Charles Schultz's *Peanuts* cartoons, Lucy marches up to Schroeder and says, "Guess what ... If you don't tell me that you love me, you know what I'm going to do? I'm going to hold my breath until I pass out!" Looking up from his piano, Schroeder says, "Breath-holding in children is an interesting phenomenon. It could indicate a metabolic disorder ... A forty-milligram dose of Vitamin B6 twice a day might be helpful ... I think that's probably it ... You need B6 ... You might consider eating more bananas, avocados, and beef liver." As Schroeder goes back to his piano, Lucy sighs, "I ask for love, and all I get is beef liver!"

For most of us, life has delivered experiences like Lucy's. All we want is to be loved, and sometimes the important people in our lives deliver beef liver. It's helpful then to step inside our heart and start to pray for whoever delivered the beef liver, wishing for them all the good things we wish for ourselves—the key to freedom through divine love expressed as forgiveness.

I'm remembering my friend Sally. She hated her mother and couldn't be in the same room with her anymore. Her tender heart had been deeply hurt as a child by things her mother said and did. Her mother was a brilliant nurse who had become a drug addict. Growing up, Sally didn't realize her mother was an addict. What she did realize was that her mother's behavior was terribly erratic, so much so that she never wanted to bring friends home. As a child, she often had to prepare the meals and care for her younger brother. Each year her resentment grew. When I met Sally, her resentment was so intense she could barely speak to her mother without becoming enraged.

The thought of loving her mother seemed impossible. She didn't even want to try. Forgiveness seemed not only impossible but undesirable. Sally's horizons began to close in on her until the pain of unforgiveness and resentment was worse than the idea of actually forgiving her mom and releasing the resentment. She became willing to pray for her mother, wishing for her mom all the good things she wished for herself. The miracle happened only a few months later. She told me one day, "I talked to my mom today and felt compassion for her." Sally's willingness to forgive her mom opened the door for the power of divine love to be activated in her. She began to know a new freedom and peace as a result. As Erasmus said, "Bidden or not bidden, God is present." Call it what you will—God, Divine Energy, the Universe, Source. God as the creative, unifying, healing energy of love is always present and when bidden is activated to heal what needs healing and to attract greater good—with astonishing precision.

It has been said that love is a decision we make and may be one of our most important life decisions. Love is both a noun and a verb—a state of heart and an action that expresses what is in the heart. It is a powerful emotion that ignites our imagination and urges expression. Love energy inspires extraordinary courage, generosity, and kindness.

My friend Julie's mom was a pistol—irreverent and downright ornery. A couple of years ago her health deteriorated to the point where she needed constant care. Julie and her sister began the vigil as caretakers. I heard about the challenges regularly, the biggest one being that their mom didn't want the help she needed. Yet in the midst of her mother's demands and deprecations, Julie managed to maintain a sense of humor and tended her mother with loving-kindness.

It is these difficult experiences that draw us into a love that is infinitely more than our humanness would allow or even choose. The flame of divine love unceasingly yearns to spread its healing, empowering warmth in the midst of all the winters of our lives. It is the enriching summer sun that allows people and dreams to flower into their inherent, exquisite beauty.

Life consistently offers opportunities to stretch our hearts, ever increasing our capacity to love until it reaches its full potential— unconditional and unstoppable, all-encompassing and breathtakingly creative. Love focuses our imagination on what we deeply desire rather than on our problems.

Valentine's Day has a long history dating back to the Roman Empire. While it has evolved throughout the centuries, the theme is still love. I remember bringing Valentine's Day cards for all my classmates in my early grade school days and making valentines for my parents each year. In fact, my own children did the same thing for me and I have their cards still—every one of them. I keep them in a special drawer and every once in a while reread those treasures. Each time I get teary and smile in my heart. I am filled again with the priceless joy that comes from those expressions of their love. The media and merchants, while often maligned for marketing love, do a great service in reminding us of the importance of expressing our love and caring for one another in concrete ways.

If we are lucky, we each have a treasury of love stories tucked away in our hearts. Any time is a good time to bring them out and let their bejeweled wonders light our hearts once again, giving us a renewed passion to take up the quest for making love more concrete and dynamic in our daily lives.

Revisiting them reminds us of the remarkable power of love: mender of hearts, nectar of joy, vitamin of faith and hope, fire of creative expression, igniter of courage, grounding of purpose, birther of vision, and breath of life. Why not take a few minutes now and invite your own love stories to bless and inspire you? Let their beauty remind you of your own and how sweet life can be when seasoned with expressions of love.

The HeartMath Institute in Boulder Creek, California, has been researching the intelligence of the heart since the early 1990s. Their mission is to help individuals and organizations reduce stress and its negative impact on physical, emotional, and relationship health. Their goal is to empower people to choose the way of love.

Throughout the years, they have experimented with various psychological and physiological measures. What they found is that the variability of the heart rate was an accurate reflection of inner emotional states and stress levels. The tests consistently demonstrated that negative emotions led to disorder in the heart's rhythms with a consequent negative impact on the overall health of the body. They found positive emotions created increased harmony and coherence in the body. Less stress equals happier body, equals happier person.

Their research also discovered that when people shift their feelings from negative to positive, their brain waves change accordingly. When we feel joy, peace, or love, the brain generates a very different wave pattern than when we are stuck in anger, irritation, or judgment. All the little and big ways of expressing love bless others while contributing to our own health, vitality, and peace. HeartMath's research demonstrated the way of love is the way to better health, creativity, emotional balance, and personal effectiveness.

That's what Father Edwin Leahy, whom you met in an earlier chapter, did for the boys at St. Benedict's Prep. He inspired boys who didn't love themselves or their lives to come to love and value one another and, as a result, to respect themselves. One of the school mottos expresses an understanding of divine love: "Whatever hurts my brother hurts me." Life at St. Benedict's is one of discipline. The boys are expected to study, to be on time, to respect one another, and to support one another to express their best. Love disciplines in the same way. Divine love thrives in forgiveness, appreciation, gratitude, compassion, thoughtfulness, kindness, and generosity. That takes positive discipline, such as expressing appreciation when you would much rather be appreciated. Activating divine love is a top-notch spiritual fitness program.

The disciple John is the biblical exemplar of love. The energetic center of love is right there in your heart of hearts. Love vibrates pink. Just as our heart pumps life to all parts of our body, thoughts, words, and expressions of love pump vitality and joy to every part of our being and our life.

Take a little time today and open the treasure chest of your own sweet experiences of being loved and giving love. Let memories of kindness, appreciation, and generosity minister to you. Remember that thoughts are things, and those memories generate positive energy and spiritual power.

One of my sweet memories is of phone calls to my dad after my mom's death. He was so lonely he just wanted to die. He did not want to go on living without her. I would call every Saturday, hoping to alleviate some of his loneliness. He would always close our conversation with, "Thank you for calling, sweetie pie. I've loved you since the day you were born." Even in his grief, or maybe because of it, his heart was softened and healed by his fond memories of loving moments. The spiritual power of love is the nectar of God within us ministering to us in every needed and desired way. Because of that, our love ministers to others.

AFFIRM LOVE

- *I think loving thoughts, and my loving thoughts attract loving experiences.*

- *I am a beacon of divine love in the world. I radiate love and magnetize love.*

- *I apprentice myself to love, and love blesses me and all my relationships with peace and joy.*

VISUALIZE LOVE

Take some deep, long breaths, and rest easy in your body. Rest your mind in your heart and hold this thought: *Divine love is filling my heart and expanding it to hold more love.* Gently close your eyes and reflect on all of your favorite things and all the people you love. Embrace the thought that divine love is anointing your body with its healing, life-giving, shimmering pink light. In your mind's eye, see this brilliant, sparkling, pulsating pink light expand with your breath to fill your body. Feel a sense of happy anticipation in the thought that the power of love is blessing your life, enlivening your body, empowering your heart's desires, and guiding your thoughts and actions into the miracles of love. Hold the idea that love is creating a magnetic field within and around you, drawing miracles and beautiful blessings into your life now.

PRAY LOVE

God of infinite beauty and magnificence, you awaken me to the mystery and miracle of being here and to the quiet immensity of your presence in me. You guide me to cross the new frontiers of love that beckon, you lead me to discover and express the best in me, you warm my heart with beautiful thoughts and a willingness to love unflinchingly.

PRACTICE LOVE

1. For the next 21 days, pray for anyone you need to forgive or who you think needs to forgive you. Put yourself at the top of the list. Wish for each one all the good things you wish for yourself. Resolve to grow in self-esteem by doing estimable things.

2. Send a "love you" text to someone you love—family member, friend.

3. Practice these three A's: Acknowledge, Appreciate, Applaud.

    a. Acknowledge someone today for their good efforts.

    b. Either verbally or in writing, appreciate someone today.

    c. Congratulate someone today for something they have accomplished. The more we applaud others' successes, the more our successes are applauded.

REFLECT ON LOVE

1. Reflect for a moment to see whether there is anyone you need to forgive or who needs to forgive you. (See the practices above.)

2. What are some of the ways you express love? Appreciate the power of love being active in you this week.

3. Who and what are you grateful for? Gratitude ignites your love power and is an expression of it.

Chapter 11
Imagination: Divine Design

That man has latent possibilities goes without argument, and that there is a limit to the ability of the mind is unthinkable. What a man imagines he can do, that he can do ... To allow the imagination to drift in daydreams never brings anything to pass. Ideas must be worked up into living, breathing, thinking things.

—Charles Fillmore, *Christian Healing*

I became a single mom when my children were 3 and 4 years old. I was terrified at first. How would I support us? How could I work full-time and still be the kind of mom I wanted to be? I realized I had to go back to work and began to imagine what kind of job I would like. I began to envision being a flight attendant, a dream I courted all through college. Back then, I would visualize all the alluring places around the world I wanted to visit. I saw myself at the Trevi Fountain in Rome, driving the Amalfi Coast in Italy, and basking in the sun on tropical islands with white sand beaches, coconut palms, and fragrant plumeria everywhere. I visualized myself meditating to flute music at the Great Pyramid of Giza. I married my college sweetheart instead.

Seven years later as a single mom, the dream walked itself back into my imagination. I decided to apply for a job as a flight attendant but was rejected. Women with small children were not accepted at the time. I was outraged by what felt like prejudice. However, anger turned to grieving as I watched a dream die—at least I thought.

At the time I was teaching Spanish in an Adult and Continuing Education Program in suburban Chicago. It just so happened that two of my students were a husband and wife who worked for TWA. Fred was a pilot and Judy was a flight attendant. One evening I shared with them my desire to work for the airlines and what had happened. Just a couple of weeks later, they walked into class with an application for one of the airlines that happened to be hiring reservationists. I had not even thought of that, but God had. My imagination was on fire again. I applied and was accepted. My prayers were answered although not in the way I had envisioned. Still my prayers and all those visualizations magnetized the circumstances—which I could not have imagined with my own knowledge—that opened the way to working for the airlines and flying for free with airline passes.

This is the power of imagination: See your heart's desire, feel it, pray it, and seek guidance while trusting the Universe. I know it is easier said than done to let go and trust, to accept disappointments and move forward. Our minds naturally want to figure it out and try as best we can to control the outcome. And then, of course, we want what we want *now*!

Reflect for a moment on the dearest dreams of your heart. What are the visions that excite your heart today? The truth is that, at their core, in their purest form, they are God-given.

Your imagination is your capacity to form pictures in your mind's eye. It is said to be the architect and builder of our dreams, the scissors of the mind, our invisible paintbrush and palette of colors.

Your imagination generates, for better or for worse, the living pictures of your thoughts. Our main task in creating the kind of life we want to live is to choose, with exquisite care and attention, the pictures that occupy the canvas of our mind. Pictures held in our mind with matching emotions in our heart create after their kind. Mixed messages from mind and heart produce mixed results. Mixed emotions are truly negative potions.

Your imagination, in concert with your faith, shapes substance. It clothes your thoughts with form and color. What you see affects how you are and what you do. To catch God's vision for our lives, we need to divinize our imaginations by refusing to allow fears, self-limiting thoughts, or painful memories be the films we project on the screen of our minds.

It can happen when we go after a dream, when we face the unknown, or when we've gotten bad news about the stock market, our children, or our jobs. Just for a moment, reflect on a time when your imagination created a worst-case scenario. One scary thought led to another and another and pretty soon your body responded and your thinking went into jumping jack mode.

My friend Cindy, upon hearing that her son Ryan, a freshman at Northwestern University, had been suspended for drinking on campus, engaged her imagination to envision a spiral of failure. Vivid pictures of Ryan's failing his classes as a result of the suspension loomed. That picture morphed into his being expelled. Next, her father would be outraged. It wasn't long before Cindy's alarm became panic. Fortunately, she reached out for prayer support. We began to scrutinize her worst-case scenario for what it was—fear running rampant. We prayed, envisioning Ryan back in school next semester and back to being the smart, good kid he had always been. A calm came over Cindy, then even a smile appeared. A positive vision led to a positive emotional response.

What would it be like for you to be creatively fearless? What pictures come to mind? You have a unique artistry. Your imagination plays a crucial role in bringing that artistry to the world. For example, the University of California San Diego created an exciting department called the Arthur C. Clarke Center for Human Imagination. Arthur C. Clarke was a science innovator, a visionary science fiction writer, a man ahead of his time as an environmentalist, and an inspiration to everyone who knew him. Here in this interdisciplinary research laboratory, named in honor of the contributions of Clarke's visionary imagination, researchers explore the nature of creativity. The center integrates the arts, sciences, humanities, engineering, and medicine, exploring the basis of imagination itself.

Interestingly, they "imagine" their work will stimulate and harness our human imagination. Among the goals of the center is to find effective ways to use imagination in education and in finding solutions to humanity's problems: "We aim to press the limits of the possible, finding new ways to understand and enrich the human experience." What would it look like if you were to press the limits of what you currently think is possible?

Spirituality has been advocating for this for a very long time. Jesus claimed that we could perform greater miracles than he did. There are right now and have been all along reliable spiritual tools for stimulating and harnessing our imagination. Through prayer and meditation, a mysterious activity ensues. It seems that out of nowhere an idea comes to mind that energizes us. Embracing the idea fires up our imagination, which paints a picture of what that idea would look like fulfilled.

During one of my long-imagined moves to San Diego to finally live near my two adult children, my friend Alisha gave me a book called *LifeLaunch: A Passionate Guide to the Rest of Your Life* by Pamela D. McLean and Frederic M. Hudson (Hudson Institute, 2011). Hudson's story helped keep my imagination tethered to positive possibilities. Hudson had contracted polio at age 9 and thought his life was over. However, his nurse, Susan, awakened his imagination to creating an enlivening vision. She taught him that he was not powerless and could create what he wanted with his thoughts.

Susan suggested that Frederic look up to the ceiling and envision a bright future. She convinced him that if he would practice seeing this vision on the ceiling, he would actually see it happen. He believed her and practiced diligently. He eventually left the hospital and learned to walk again. He went on to graduate from Columbia University with a Ph.D. in philosophy. Happy ending? Not yet.

He was teaching at the University of San Francisco and found himself without a vision (read: purpose) for his life. He had accomplished all the goals that he and Susan had imagined together. Wisely, he called Susan and asked her for advice. She told him to gaze up at the sky just as he had gazed at the ceiling years earlier to get a new vision on where he wanted to go and why. She suggested he once again find the fire of passion and hope he had found in that hospital room. He created a drawing board in the sky, inviting a beautiful vision to emerge containing a purpose that fired his passion and stirred his spirit. An inspiring vision, in fact, did emerge and he went on to take it from the sky of his mind to the reality of a powerful leadership and coaching organization called the Hudson Institute of Coaching.

My son Eddie's imagination was supported and empowered early on by special moments with my dad. Growing up in Chicago meant long, cold, and very white winters. Shoveling snow became a regular routine in early December and continued through March and even into April. When Eddie was just a toddler, one of his favorite things to do was "help" his grandpa shovel snow.

Dressed in his navy snowsuit with white boots, red mittens, and a checkered woolen scarf tied snugly around his neck, covering his little chin and lips, he would follow along behind my dad. Dad would push the shovel, and Eddie would push his little plastic yellow lawn mower. It was always summertime for Eddie, even in the midst of harsh winter conditions. His eyes sparkled with joy as he moved forward through the snowy coldness with his lawn mower, a symbol of sweet summer. My dad would commend him for being such a great helper and brag about him at the family dinners that followed the shoveling adventures. Eddie's imagination was ignited with visions of making a difference on the playing field of his life. For him, winter is still full of summertime.

Even in the winters of our lives, we can fill our imagination with summer—unfrozen dreams and possibilities. We can follow in the footsteps of the divine presence, creating a summertime frame of mind that flourishes with colorful, fragrant opportunities. We can fire up our imagination, inviting God to reveal a beautiful thought, an encouraging picture of a positive possibility.

That's how the Chicago Cubs must have done it in 2016 when they won the World Series in the 10th inning of a nail-biting seventh game with the Cleveland Indians. *60 Minutes* aired a segment on the two men who had turned around the Cubs' 108-year losing streak. The alchemy of Manager Joe Maddon and President of Baseball Operations Theo Epstein created a culture of excellence, optimism, and mutual support and encouragement. But there was more. On that fateful day, tied 6-6 and forced into a rain delay before the 10th inning, right fielder Jason Heyward ignited the team's imagination with visions of winning, of pulling together to make it happen. Back on the field, they did just that. Those visions evoked the players' resilience. Their now-nourished imaginations fired their power, strength, and faith centers. They could see themselves winning, and a picture—even a mental picture—is worth a thousand words!

Your imagination is a miracle-working tool for creating inner pictures that guide your steps to make those visions real in your circumstances. What you see on the screen of your mind can be a magnet that draws the necessary resources to manifest the vision. Imagination is our interior filmmaker, and we always have a choice about which films we produce. What would it be like if you banished fear and all the self-limiting pictures your fears produce? What would it be like if you banished regret and resentment and all the painful pictures they produce?

In her 1921 book *Your Invisible Power*, Genevieve Behrend writes, "Your mental picture is the force of attraction which evolves and combines the Originating Substance into specific shape."

Our imaginations, when purified of negative perspectives, catch the divine vision planted in us. With your imagination fired, your heart catches fire, too, and there is nothing you cannot do. Start now to imagine the best for yourself. God could not want less.

Remember the Langston Hughes poem from earlier? It describes the work of imagination as well:

Hold fast to dreams
For if dreams die
Life is a broken-winged bird
That cannot fly.

Hold fast to dreams
For when dreams go
Life is a barren field
Frozen with snow.

Your imagination is a divine dream catcher and architect.

AFFIRM IMAGINATION

- *I am the architect of my life, and I intend to create a masterpiece.*

- *I envision the best and delete the rest.*

- *I imagine good, and good happens.*

VISUALIZE IMAGINATION

Close your eyes and take a deep, long breath. Let your robust breath fill your whole being. Imagine you are breathing in shimmering white light from the infinite resources of the Universe. Breathe the white light through your whole being, clearing and blessing the canvas of your mind for an energizing vision of good. In your mind's eye, see a sparkling light-blue light, the light of imagination, right behind and in the middle of your physical eyes. Watch this sky-blue light begin to expand to fill you with its shimmering radiance. Breathe this brilliant, iridescent blue light into every cell and atom of your being. Now into the creative power of divine imagination, place a desire of your heart. See your desire take form. Picture it as clearly and in as much detail as you can. Love the picture. Smile into the picture. Now, give thanks that this awesome picture of your heart's desire is outpicturing in your life. Watch for clues as to next right steps.

PRAY IMAGINATION

Great and magnificent Architect, holder of a divine plan for my life, I give thanks that I can catch a vision of the amazing good possible for me. I release all veils that block my clear view of the exciting possibilities for my relationships, career, health, finances, and creative expression. You now set my feet upon the path to fulfill the divine visions that live in me. Amen.

PRACTICE IMAGINATION

1. Wear something light blue for 21 days with the intention of focusing your imagination on the good you seek.

2. Memorize the affirmations or keep them in your hip pocket to bring out and replace any negative thoughts.

3. Create a vision board (pictures and words) of your heart's desire and put it where you will see it each day. It's a consciousness conditioner and impacts your imagination with its depictions of your heart's desires.

REFLECT ON IMAGINATION

1. If you were to give yourself a "rain delay" pep talk that fired up your imagination, what would you say? What would you go back out and do on the playing field of your life?

2. What do you do to nourish your imagination and creativity?

3. Who is a role model who inspires your imagination to dare new things?

Chapter 12

Wisdom: Astonishing Clarity

The wisdom from above is first pure, then peaceable, gentle, open to reason, full of mercy and good fruits, without uncertainty or insincerity.

—James 3:17 (RSV)

Divine wisdom, the wisdom from "above," is centered in our solar plexus and, not accidentally, close to the heart. It vibrates yellow like a glorious sun in the early morning hours. It is grounded in faith and understanding and filtered through love. It rightly advises our choices and actions. It is the power to discern life-enhancing values. The exemplar for wisdom is the disciple James, brother of John who represents love. Wisdom integrated with love, and vice versa, yields the best possible decision and action.

One of my first spiritual teachers would respond to my muddled thinking about my marriage by saying, "When you don't know, don't." It was comforting to be relieved of having to figure it out and force a solution, which usually didn't work out well anyway. He went on to say, "Spirit never speaks in confused tones. Spirit always speaks in a way that you can understand." This is divine wisdom made practical. My teacher gave me a mantra to use while waiting for clarity: "I know what to do, and I do it." Try it when you have an important decision to make and you aren't sure which way to go or what choice to make. Listen to your thoughts and watch for clues that are meant to guide you.

The human perspective rushes us, pressures us to do something or avoid doing anything. The human mind is incredibly anxious about the unknown. It wants answers and wants them now. For this reason, our thinking will incline us to force a solution. We will want to make something happen or conversely push the avoidance button. Divine wisdom, however, is discerning and results in clarity regarding next right steps. Wisdom marries the facts of life with spiritual principles. Like King Solomon, it is the judge that sees beyond appearances, senses the truth in the midst of circumstances, separating with uncommon accuracy the wheat of life from the chaff. Divine wisdom walks the path of immense compassion in the direction of peace, wearing shoes of spiritual principle.

My friend Cheri felt stale and frustrated in her career as a minister. She had invested 10 years and now was acutely dissatisfied with her income and the growth of her congregation. Like many of us, when we are dissatisfied in our work or personal life and don't know what to do, she tried a scattershot approach. She began to try one thing after another. She then concluded that she ought to look for greener pastures.

She tried that, too, only to discover the pasture wasn't greener after all. Her head hurt from no-reward efforts. In the midst of her disappointment and disillusionment, she summoned her power of wisdom. Ever so gently she began to see a new door opening, a clue. She glimpsed an even bigger possibility for her life that thrilled her heart. Now with a mind of peace, she heard an exquisitely energizing call, not away from ministry but to a bigger kind of ministry. She knew what to do and she started doing it. Today she is a wise and sought-after church consultant. When you tap into divine wisdom, you come to understand what to do and have the power and exuberance to do it.

Along those lines, I made a pact with God—I thought. I said out loud as well as silently, "I don't ever want to move again. I don't want to start over again. Enough is enough!" At the time, I lived in San Rafael, California. I loved my work in San Francisco and my home. Just across the street from my townhouse was a walking path along San Francisco Bay. I had a breathtaking view of the San Francisco skyline across the water. I had made good friends, had symphony tickets, friends to golf with, and someone to dance with. My life brimmed with good. The topper on all that good was coming face-to-face one day with Robert Redford himself—for real—while I was rollerblading in Tiburon. I spotted him sitting on a bench with a young man, his daughter's boyfriend as it turned out. I nonchalantly skated past him and, 200 feet farther, halted, got up my courage, skated back, and spoke to him as if I knew him (only in my dreams). He was quite gracious. We had a short chat and I went on my way, gleeful for having listened to my thumping heart rather than my merciless head. *It just doesn't get any better than that,* I thought. *Why would I ever consider moving? Never!* Then I learned it isn't a good idea to tell the Universe "never."

In my "never" state of mind, I began to hear a voice in my heart whispering for me to apply for a position at Unity World Headquarters in Unity Village, Missouri. For three or four months, I endeavored to hush it up. It would not be hushed. The inner voice was crystal clear. I finally surrendered and applied.

It was a pleasantly warm day at Unity Village after the interviews. I decided to go for a run along the golf course under the canopy of giant pecan trees. Halfway down the road, I heard a crisp, clear voice announcing, *You're going to love it here.* Back in San Francisco two weeks later, I said *yes* to the job offer and, over all of my previous objections, I felt a sense of peace. This is the energy and alchemy of divine wisdom—a knowing that is beyond reasons and words.

Wisdom is crystal clear about the difference between being right and doing the right thing. It culls knowledge, experience, and Truth to create the most positive, good-enhancing, and effective responses to life. It is the great judge who sits on the throne of the heart. It is trustworthy and true.

Wisdom inspires not only right action but right thinking as well. One of the things I do to support thinking "right" is to cut out inspirational stories, headlines, poems, and quotes. I keep them in a file and pull them out every once in a while when my thinking veers off course. This always seems to tap into my inner resilience.

An ad for the Bellagio hotel in Las Vegas appeared in *Time* magazine and went directly into my next Sunday talk and then into my file. It had white words jumping off a black backdrop—"Stay Legendary." It touched that forever desire to make a difference in the world. Steve Jobs put it this way, "I want to put a ding in the universe." Don't we all!

Omega watches ran this ad: "For the Olympian in us all." HP's inspirational words in their ad have been: "If you're going to do something, make it matter." Even advertisements point to our inherent ability to choose wisely and act from the best in ourselves. That is divine wisdom.

Kayla Harrison, an Olympic gold medalist in judo for the United States, the first ever for an American, had a long journey to the gold. She was sexually abused by a former coach. She said, "I hated everything … I was a teenage punk." It took awakening to something in her that was bigger than that experience, something that could lift her out of the hate. She found a gold-inspired vision that created a chink in her protective armor enough to catch a glimpse of the indwelling Olympian. There is an Olympian in you seeking to emerge. It is the spirit of God in you seeking to evolve. It's better to surrender to it, because it is relentless.

AFFIRM WISDOM

- *I know what to do, and I do it.*

- *Divine wisdom now guides me to my next right step, and I take it.*

- *Divine wisdom inspires me to take the next right step.*

VISUALIZE WISDOM

Gently close your eyes, take a deep, long breath, and picture a crystal-clear day, the sun radiating iridescent yellow light against a backdrop of a luminous, cerulean blue sky. Breathe the yellow light of the sun into your solar plexus, and in your mind's eye, see it shining and radiating there. Breathe and draw this sparkling, pulsating yellow light through your whole body from head to toe. See yourself bathed in the vibration of divine wisdom and know that it is ministering to you—spirit, soul, and body. Linger with this vision and feel its energy at work in you.

PRAY WISDOM

God of infinite wisdom, I know you are the answer to all my questions and the solution to all my problems. I give thanks that you enlighten me with right and perfect ideas and choices for my life. I open my whole being and welcome wisdom to be my compass and my fortress.

PRACTICE WISDOM

1. Wear something yellow for a week and notice the impact it has. Perhaps your thinking seems clearer? Maybe you notice intuitive hunches?

2. Use the affirmation *"I know what to do, and I do it"* like a mantra. Notice its impact.

3. Before making decisions, even simple ones, pray and ask yourself what divine wisdom would do.

REFLECT ON WISDOM

1. Think of a time when you made a difficult decision—left a job, started a job, let go of a friendship, or bought a new home. What values came to the forefront to help your decision?

2. How has wisdom informed the current priorities in your life?

3. What is the best advice (wisdom) that you have given yourself?

Chapter 13

Will: Divinely Guided Choices

Will in the mind of God is an idea of decisive action. Will in man is the
Power to act decisively.

—Ella Pomeroy, *Powers of the Soul*

Will is the decision making, directing, choosing faculty of the mind. It
is our capacity to say "yes" or "no" to opportunities and options. The
highest expression of will is willingness, conscious consent to the will of
God.

—*Metaphysics 2*

My inspiring friend Georgia had lost all hope of having
a life she could tolerate. It seemed her usual resilience
ebbed to zero. In the midst of dementia and frailty
that compelled her to depend on others and kept her homebound,
her relationship with the God of her understanding prevailed. I
think she had a conversation with the spirit of God in her, asking
to be relieved of the burden of her body. And her beautiful spirit
gracefully led her into the next dimension.

Reflect for a moment on some of the grace-filled moments in
your own life. Was there perhaps an outcome that was far better than you could have imagined on your own? Were there moments when you (finally) prayed yourself into letting Spirit take
the reins?

I learned the hard way that my life works better if I seek divine guidance. I had to admit that I often made choices based on
fears or other's opinions. Call it testing the waters, this practice

of building faith so that in prayer we actually seek divine guidance, God's will. We come to know a will greater than our human will by remembering to pray for guidance, watch for divine clues (synchronicities), and listen for the still, small voice. Divine guidance can come through people too. Our spirit will recognize it. It's letting life coach us.

Out on a walk with my friend Suzie, she asked what I planned to talk about in church that Sunday. I gave her the title—"A Well-Trained Will"—to which she responded, "Oh, that's hard. I don't have a well-trained will. I justify and rationalize stuff even though I know better. Sometimes I just don't even think about God's will." We both laughed because we both know better and often don't do better.

The *will*, called the executive power of our mind, is located behind our forehead in the frontal lobe of the brain, next to *understanding*. This area of the brain is dopamine-sensitive and associated with reward, attention, and motivation as well as voluntary movement. Projecting future consequences, problem-solving, emotional expression, and judgment are functions of the frontal lobe. As we discipline the creative energy of our will by seeking and then acting on divine guidance, all of these capacities evolve to their highest possible expression.

Lane and Sara had their wedding reception in an elegant ballroom at the Ironhorse Golf Club in Leawood, Kansas. At the west end of the ballroom was a floor-to-ceiling, wall-to-wall window overlooking the golf course. At one point during the reception, I walked over to enjoy the beautiful view of rolling green hills. Just below the window, a golfer prepared to tee off. He carefully placed his ball on the tee, picked up his club with the same diligent care, and took his stance precisely. He just as precisely adjusted his feet, bouncing a bit as he bent his knees slightly. He looked out at the flag on the green in the distance, stood back, moved behind the ball to look out in a direct line, took his stance again, repeated the adjustments and, now, well-prepared, he drew his club back over his shoulders and then in a flash brought the club down to smack the ball straight down the fairway. As I watched this ritual, I thought, *What loving care, what disciplined practice, what clear intention. What a well-trained will!*

I also thought it was excellent advice for my own will—to see the practice it takes to play the game of life by divine instruction, what it takes to practice restraint of tongue and pen, to take the lemons that life serves up and make lemonade.

Will is the great permission-giver. It gives permission to all of our other powers to take action. It moves our other 11 creative energies into action. Still, the most important decision we can make is to be willing toward divine will, with the understanding that divine will is magnanimously benevolent. Human will would like for God to take away hardships and difficulties, but these are our spiritual growing edges. The divine presence within equips us to overcome the difficulties and hardships.

My daughter Jennifer called me sobbing one February afternoon. Through the choking sobs, I heard, "Mom, I'm pregnant again. How could this happen? We've been practicing birth control, and the doctor said the baby is a boy, maybe twins!" She and her husband John had talked about *maybe* having another baby, but if they ever were to do it, they wanted a girl. They already had two healthy little boys only 13 months apart.

Her will was clearly not to have another baby unless it would be a girl. She struggled with this fact of her life—not only pregnant again but with a boy. She wasn't finding any willingness there. She wasn't even looking for it, at least not yet. She agreed to pray. An ounce of willingness trickled in, along with a mustard seed of faith that this, while not her plan, might be God's plan, that maybe this baby wanted *her* for his mother.

Nine months later a beautiful baby boy arrived, and Jennifer couldn't have been happier. Her small ounce of willingness toward God's will was transformed into peace and then profound joy. Now a remarkable young man, Braedon still delights her and makes her so grateful to be his mom.

The Bible is full of examples of our human tendency to resist what we don't want and fight as if fighting it would change what is. Take Jonah. He was clear that God was guiding him to go to Nineveh to teach the people about the one God. He was also clear that he did not want to go. He carried on a vigorous internal argument with God. Big mistake. Argue with what we know we must do, and we strand ourselves in a no-man's-land—like being trapped in the stomach of a whale as Jonah was.

Fighting what is or what we know in our heart we ought to do is a sure sign that our will is driving our thinking. When we become willing to accept what is, the door to creative solutions opens. We make a space for grace. The same is true for doing the right thing, as difficult as it may seem.

Consistently aligning our will with divine will is not done quickly. It results from patient, persistent spiritual study, prayer, and meditation so that we can recognize divine guidance when we hear it. It is worth every effort we make, though, because we come to experience a peace that surpasses all understanding and a joy that cannot be taken from us. Being willing opens the doors of heaven.

Because our will moves the other creative powers, a spiritually trained will is crucial. Imagine choosing a teenager to be president of the country or to run a large corporation. Unthinkable as that is, it is just as ill-advised to count on our untrained will to make the best decisions, especially in difficulties. It will depend on the level of our spiritual knowledge and understanding. We grow our capacity to make spiritually guided choices in a holistic way by developing our 12 powers through prayer, study, meditation, and practice.

Surrendering to divine will is not weak. It is not the same at all as giving up. It creates an opening for divine ideas. Divine ideas are the most powerful things in the universe. They are recognizable by their goodness and capacity to heal, build relationships, enhance our sense of well-being, and maximize our enjoyment of life.

Myra Thompson radiated vitality that day. She felt on top of the world because, after a lot of effort to become an ordained minister, she got word that she had received her license to preach. She was off to Emanuel AME Church in Charleston, South Carolina, that evening to lead her Bible study group. It was her first official act. She never came home. Neither did eight others.

Dylann Roof, a 21-year-old described as a white supremacist and domestic terrorist, came to her Bible study group that evening. He was warmly welcomed. He listened to the sharing, disagreeing periodically. When the group went into prayer, he rose, pulled a Glock .45-caliber handgun from his backpack, and gunned down nine African Americans point-blank. How does Myra's husband, Rev. Anthony Thompson, forgive? He *chooses* to forgive. In David Von Drehle's 2015 *Time* article, Rev. Thompson shared that he chose to forgive for his own freedom. He said, "When I forgave him, my peace began ... I'm done with him. He doesn't have control of me." Rev. Thompson knows resentment and hatred are not part of God.

We have been horrified before and since by unthinkable acts of violence—one human being destroying lives by choice. Yet in the midst of irreparable loss, the hearts of the loved ones of those murdered *are* repaired by the power of choice, by the action of seeking divine help. They refuse to allow their hearts to be eaten up with the rage they must have felt.

Peter came to Jesus hoping for some justification for not forgiving, for some exceptions. He asked, "Lord, how often shall my brother sin against me, and I forgive him? As many as seven times?" (Matthew 18:21 RSV)

You might think that seven times would be beyond the call of duty. But Jesus responded, "I do not say to you seven times, but seventy times seven" (Matthew 18:22 RSV). In other words, forgive until you don't have to anymore, until the emotional charge of the offense is no longer there. The fact of the incident remains, but freedom has been won by seeking to align with the will of God, which Jesus taught in this instance is forgiveness.

Jesus addressed the depth and power of forgiveness in his own torturous experience when he said, "Father, forgive them; for they do not know what they are doing" (Luke 23:34). He called on the grace of God to forgive through him.

Rev. Anthony Thompson and all who have been affected by acts of violence but have exercised their will to be willing to forgive, taste the freedom Jesus and other spiritual masters and teachers promise. In choosing to forgive, we ascend in consciousness to a whole new level of freedom.

We don't have to and are ill-served by depending on our own strengths and wits to handle the difficulties as well as opportunities that demand our best. We can turn to the indwelling spirit of God and be resourced to rise out of life's difficulties.

A preeminent metaphysics teacher and one of the most provocative teachers I had in seminary was Rev. Ed Rabel. I once heard him say that the only use any of us had to make of our human will was to surrender it to God. I actually felt an indescribable sense of relief when I heard that, since I believed I had to figure everything out by my own wits. Still, hearing it filled me with great consternation. At the time, I had no idea how to surrender my will to a power greater than myself, namely God. While I thought it would be a relief not to have to figure everything out for myself, down deep I was worried that God's will might definitely be something I didn't want, even though I had certainly been getting inconsistent to horrible results making choices on my own.

The mantra of my prayers resembled what I found in an anonymous quote, "I desperately need some wise advice, which will recommend that I do what I want to do." However, I began an experiment in building trust. I started praying for divine guidance with small things. I also began meditating as a practice each day—making a space for grace, I was told.

Why not perform your own experiment? Meditate each day, asking for God's will, listening for the still, small voice, and then taking action on what you perceive to be God's will for you.

Jesus said it clearly, "I seek not my own will but the will of him who sent me" (John 5:30 RSV). He suggested that if we, too, follow this way of living, we will be living in the kingdom of heaven on earth. The one who sent Jesus also sends us with a mission to maximize our spiritual potential, which must result in a life well-lived and enjoyed! This call is embedded in the very cellular structure of our being. And if we are willing, we will be divinely guided to its fulfillment.

Mountain climber Jim Whittaker, the first American to reach the summit of Mount Everest, said, "You don't conquer mountains ... you conquer yourself." Being willing for and seeking God's will makes the climb graceful.

How can you come to know God's will for you?

1. Let your inner mantra be *"God's will is for good at all times and in all places."*

2. Ask for God's will in simple things at first.

3. Know the language of Spirit:

   - It's clear. If unclear, it's not Spirit.
   - It is pure, peaceable, gentle, open-minded, full of mercy.
   - It produces positive results.
   - It is without uncertainty or insincerity.

AFFIRM WILL

- *My willingness for God's will generates miracles.*
- *Every day in every way I seek God's will and follow divine guidance.*
- *My divinely guided choices stretch me and grow me into the greatness within me.*

VISUALIZE WILL

Take a deep, head-to-toe breath, then another. In your mind's eye, see a silver light behind your forehead. As you breathe, see the shimmering silver light expand to fill your whole being. Linger with this vision, watching the spiraling, sparkling silver light, knowing that you rest in the assurance that God's will for you is always and everywhere an increase of good. What would it look like to be living in the good you seek? See that good, feel the feelings you would have in living it, and give thanks for its unfolding now. Breathe deeply and give thanks that God's goodwill is revealed to you with clarity, step by step.

PRAY WILL

Dear God, I breathe into your light within me with happy anticipation that you are guiding me this day into being the person you would have me be and into the good you would have me do. I rest in the joy that you are, and I breathe in joyous thoughts. Your joy enlivens and encourages me now. I go gratefully into my day.

PRACTICE WILL

1. Start each day with a prayer, dedicating your will to expressing the divine will. Ask to be shown throughout the day how you can express the best in you.

2. Wear silver each day for 21 days as an affirmation that divine will is guiding you into beautiful, fulfilling days and the best choices.

3. If you find yourself resisting or fighting what is, let go into being willing for divine will to guide you.

REFLECT ON WILL

1. Do you trust the God of your understanding enough to ask for good in all areas and circumstances of your life?

2. Is there a place in your life where you are fighting what is? Are you willing to let go and be open to divine guidance for a next right step?

3. Is there a circumstance in which you are trying to force a solution, pressing for what you want, and trying to control an outcome? Are you willing to let go and let God?

Chapter 14
Order: Invite Synchronicity

The divine law of order working in the subconsciousness unearths buried talents, reveals hidden powers, and paves the way for their expression. The divine law of order coordinates the mind powers so that new inspirations may come forth and find unhindered recognition ... in the conscious mind. The divine law of order emphasizes the overcoming power of man, thereby abolishing fear and despair.
—Cora Fillmore, *Christ Enthroned in Man*

Man can never exercise dominion until he knows who and what he is and, knowing, brings forth that knowledge into the external by exercising it in divine order, which is mind, idea, and manifestation.

—Charles Fillmore, *The Twelve Powers of Man*

As a preteen, I developed warts on the ball of my right foot. I probably wouldn't have noticed them except that it really hurt when I walked. Once discovered and relayed to my mom, regular trips to the podiatrist ensued to have them torched off. Throughout the years they were burned off, dug out, excavated, and medicated! The torture never did the trick, however. Sooner or later, the warts returned. I never got a clear answer as to what was causing them, nor was I ever given hope that I would be cured of them once they were fried into nothingness. This went on all throughout high school and into adulthood.

The miracle occurred while I was studying for the ministry. It happened in the "Life of Prayer" class taught by Rev. Marvin Anderson. He told us that the project for the semester would be of our choosing but that it must be a personal healing project using any two of the 12 powers. I picked something where results—or no results—would be unmistakable: the warts, which like clockwork had returned.

For the experiment, I set out to create a systematic practice that included daily visualization of the colors and the qualities of the two powers I chose—order and understanding. I practiced seeing the warts shrink while bathed in the colors.

Divine order vibrates as emerald green and divine understanding as gold. The foot is said to represent understanding. Divine order is a sorting-out kind of energy that focalizes right outcomes, right action, right thinking, right emotions. It rights whatever needs righting.

My prayer practice included daily visualization of the colors and their divine expression vibrantly active in my foot and in my beliefs, known and unknown. I would visualize the ball of my foot, where the warts kept returning, filled with the golden light of divine understanding and the emerald green power of divine order.

My practice also included time each morning and evening sitting quietly, visualizing the light of these powers like laser beams flooding my foot and dissolving the warts. I would see the ball of my foot free and smooth. I repeated affirmations: *Divine order is healing my foot now, righting what needs to be righted and releasing what needs to be released. I release all misunderstandings about myself, others, and my life.*

Because divine understanding transforms beliefs that diminish us and our sense of well-being, I became willing to change my beliefs and to see with new eyes. Meanwhile, behind the scenes, divine order apparently was making essential adjustments in my body as well as my consciousness.

I never checked the results during those 12 weeks. By the end of the semester, the warts had disappeared as if by magic and have never returned. I don't know for sure, of course, but I have come to believe that this system is the paradigm that allowed Jesus to be transfigured on the mountaintop in the presence of Peter, James, and John, when his clothes became dazzling white (Mark 9:2-3). The 12 powers vibrate as light—light energy. When the powers of faith, wisdom, and love peaked spiritually, Jesus emanated light. We say of some people that they light up a room. Their energy is so purified that they actually do seem to light up a room.

Convinced as I was of the miracle-working power of these creative energies, I developed a 12-power litany that I used like a meditation each morning (and still do many years later). I'd go from head to foot, visualizing each power as a radiant, colored light in each of the 12 areas of my body. I'd see it spiraling and expanding to fill my whole body, affirming that it was cleansing, renewing, rejuvenating, and enlightening me. I would imagine the light becoming sparkling and luminous, dissolving self-defeating beliefs. I'm still engaged with this practice and am still convinced that a spiritual alchemy has been taking place in me. I hope you will prove it for yourself.

Divine order is the idea of harmonious progress. It is the innate urge to grow always toward a more balanced and happy life. It is also a healing principle of organizations, groups, and individuals. It harmonizes the 11 other powers to produce the best possible outcome.

I've heard it said that divine order is the first law of heaven. It is the inherent capacity to perceive and cooperate with the laws of growth. It is essential for right outcomes. It is the mantle of harmonious progress.

Divine order is to fulfillment and right outcomes in life as yeast is to flour for bread. It is the matrix in which the creative process weaves its magic. Divine order, when invoked in faith, will order the circumstances of your life in the most astounding ways. You can use it like a mantra when you meet challenges, difficulties, confusion, or lack of clarity, and things will begin to right themselves. A door will open. A solution will be found.

When my daughter was a teenager, I couldn't bear to walk into her bedroom. Her clothes were everywhere except hung up in the closet or put away in a drawer. One could not walk from the doorway to the bed, a three-to-four-foot distance, without stepping on blouses, slacks, socks, or shoes. It was a mystery walk. *Could she make it to the bed without tripping over some hidden article of clothing on the floor?* I wondered. I would say that it was almost complete chaos except that the bed had not been overturned. Other choices she was making were equally undisciplined.

Sometimes our thinking can be chaotic as we try to figure out solutions to our dilemmas, whether in a relationship, health, career, or finances—or try to make the unknown future known right now. Fears mix with positive and negative possibilities and we can't see the forest for the trees. Our thoughts are as scattered as my daughter was with her clothes. We lose sight of our hopes and dreams.

Working with the energy of divine order is disciplining not only the mind and choices but our actions as well. It orders our priorities in such a way that we see clearly that our spiritual fitness comes first. Why? Because when we are spiritually fit, we are more available for divine guidance. Spiritually fit, we hear what we need to hear, both internally and through what others may say. God really does speak through others. Putting our relationship with God first is the starting point. It means a committed prayer and meditation practice.

Branch Rickey, the Brooklyn Dodgers' general manager at the time, signed Jackie Robinson despite opposition and threats on every side. Rickey told Robinson that he would break new ground for Black people, but he would have to be willing to exhibit unprecedented courage and strength in the face of insults and even abuse that would come to him as the first Black player in Major League Baseball.

Robinson did just that, albeit often with great difficulty. Sure, he loved the game of baseball and the opportunity to play in the major leagues. Even so, I have to believe that he found the idea of breaking ground for Black people a worthy cause that fired up his resilience in the face of significant difficulties.

In 1947, he was named Rookie of the Year. Only two years later, he won the National League Most Valuable Player award. His resilient spirit made a game-changing difference both on and off the field. In 2004, the first annual Jackie Robinson Day was declared, and every player on every team now wears his retired number—42—on that day in honor of his immense, immeasurable contribution to the game he loved and to the world.

This is divine order elegantly matured and active in an individual's life. We may not achieve what Jackie Robinson achieved, but in the fields of life in which we walk, we can make an equally significant contribution through our allegiance to the highest and best in ourselves, the divine presence within us, and give it room to order our thinking, feelings, and actions.

My dear friend Faith passed away in early 2008 after four years of striving with a disease that slowly atrophied her brain. Little by little she lost her capacities. But it never atrophied her spirit. The people in her congregation adored her. She would often go where angels feared to tread, advocating for civil rights, children's rights, and religious tolerance.

After 9/11, she was the first in her community to reach out to the Muslim population. She extended a hand of friendship, compassion, and consolation. In her last days, the interfaith community would come daily to her home to be in her presence. Members of the Brahma Kumaris spiritual organization came at first weekly and then daily to sprinkle rose water on her body and anoint her. Her partner in ministry and beloved husband said, "She never saw herself as anything but a servant of God."

This divinely ordered relationship with her God brought people from around the country to her memorial service, more than 1,000 strong. Putting God first is the great maximizer of our lives and divine order in expression.

The disciple James, referred to as James the Lesser, is the exemplar of divine order. Its energy vibrates emerald green. The center of order is located in the abdomen and intestines. Just as our body absorbs the nutrients of what we eat and releases the rest, the power of divine order absorbs the nutrients of the most helpful ideas and releases the rest. Our mental and emotional digestion is efficient, and right action naturally follows.

AFFIRM ORDER

- *I order my life with God, and God orders my life with good.*

- *I deepen my relationship with the Divine, and the Divine deepens my joy and prospers my life.*

- *As I take steps to be spiritually fit, new talents are revealed, new inspiration comes, and I am empowered to move forward in my life.*

VISUALIZE ORDER

Close your eyes, breathe deeply and, in your mind's eye, walk into a vision of a summer-green meadow lined with lush trees—pine, maple, oak, and poplar. Imagine yourself walking along a path in the midst of this green splendor. Breathe in the intense scents of pine and juniper. Breathe the scents and brilliant green color into your abdomen, the seat of the creative energy of divine order. Breathe the sparkling deep green throughout your body. See this pulsating green light radiating up and down to fill your whole being from the core of you to the surface. Divine order knows what to do to bless and inform your spirit, soul, and body of right, harmonious, healing thoughts. Feel a sense of gratitude and happy expectation that this divine energy is doing what it does—ordering all aspects of your being and your life to produce the most desirable outcomes. It will right what needs to be righted, order what needs to be ordered, unblock what is blocked, and make needed connections.

PRAY ORDER

I rest in the healing, maximizing, harmonizing power of divine order, grateful for the miracles and blessings that begin to take place in me, through me, and for me now. Thank you, God, for the prosperity and synchronicity now expressing in every area of my life.

PRACTICE ORDER

1. Start your day with a prayer, invoking divine order to order your day.

2. Choose a challenge or perhaps a decision you have to make and surround it in emerald green light. Give thanks

that divine order is quickened in you, revealing all that needs to be revealed.

3. Wear emerald green as a consciousness conditioner and symbol of your readiness and embrace of revelations of divine order.

REFLECT ON ORDER

1. If divine order is harmonious growth and progress, in what areas of your life have you grown and/or progressed in the past 12 months? Five years?

2. What divine synchronicity have you noticed in your life? When were you in the right place at the right time for something wonderful to happen?

3. By what priorities do you order your days now?

Chapter 15

Release/Elimination: The Power of No

"You got to stop watering dead plants."—Anonymous

I've watered many dead plants in my life, repeating continually what didn't work the first time around. I would tell myself that this time would be different. It never was. My husband kept responding the same way as always. Or I told myself that I would stop smoking next week, next month, or when … (fill in the blank with the "necessary" circumstance), and that didn't work either. My children tried to help me by tossing a whole carton of my cigarettes into the crawl space of our home and, still unwilling to release that bad habit, I put them right back in the kitchen cabinet—up high!

If you look online for quotes on *release*, you'll find pages and pages. Apparently, many people have contemplated its importance enough to have learned something they wanted to share with the world. Most seem to be about relationships—the treasured ones and the painful ones. Still, letting go of what doesn't bring you alive can be among the most difficult things you ever have to do. I remember someone saying, "Anything I've ever let go of had claw marks on it." That's been my experience too!

Take, for instance, forgiving. My friend Susie stopped to get gas one day after work. She got out of the car, credit card in hand, pulling up the collar on her jacket to brace against the cold wind. Just as she began to insert her credit card in the slot, a car pulled up behind her. The gentleman driving leaned out the window and asked her to move her car up so he could get to the pump behind her. He was driving a big SUV. That made her even less inclined to get back into her car and pull forward. Ever so reluctantly, she fussed and cussed under her breath and angrily got back in her car and moved forward. The man gassed up and got back in his car, about to leave.

Now Susie was fuming because he didn't even say thank you. She yelled at him, "You jerk. I did you a favor and you can't even say thank you!" Apparently, he was stunned, and Susie was stopped in her tracks at her boldness. She paused, took a deep breath, and realized that to be the person she wants to be, she must apologize. Of course, that's the last thing she wanted to do. Nevertheless, she shifted her focus to the principle of forgiveness. She knew from bitter experience that she was at risk of a resentment. That would, for sure, mar her peace and happiness. She told me, "I took a deep breath, gave God my anger, and went over to the guy and apologized." The result? She drove away grateful and free with the freedom of spirit, released from the pending resentment.

The power of divine release engenders renewed resilience. It cleanses mind and heart. It shape-shifts our thinking while freeing our hearts of fears, resentments, and all manner of life-depleting emotions and memories. It is as if we wipe the hard drive of our mind clean of junk files. Gradually, our consciousness can be returned to its clear, pristine state.

The most exciting thing I know about the power of release is that it can be our spiritual eraser. The most challenging part is that when we invoke its power, it is like a spiritual Roto-Rooter. It brings up the sludge of what needs to be released—residual unfinished business, incomplete communications, unhealed hurts, unmet expectations, resentments, and regrets. It's everything we've stashed because we didn't know what to do to effectively handle it at the time. To avoid or refuse to let go of something or someone that is spiritually and energetically depleting is to create systemic congestion.

My friend Ruth had been hiding from her well-armored heart for a very long time. It all began when she was a child. Her mother was emotionally punishing. She regularly meted out harsh punishments for less-than-perfect behavior. Not surprisingly, Ruth became a psychotherapist. Her Ph.D. may have helped her describe her mother's behavior clinically, but it definitely didn't heal her heart. It didn't diminish her resentments either. Now hate had turned to stark terror because of a diagnosis Ruth had just received.

Ruth came to me after a Sunday message on forgiveness. She said, "I realize that I need to forgive my mother. She haunts me, and I'm afraid to die and encounter her in any way." Ruth had been diagnosed with cancer. That was the key that opened Pandora's box.

I told her we could do a releasing exercise if she was willing. She was. We met one afternoon in my office. I made an altar on my coffee table with a candle, holy water from the grotto in Lourdes, France, and a few sacred objects. (People from around the world come to the shrine at Lourdes for healing of all manner of physical, emotional, intellectual, and spiritual maladies. The day I was there, hundreds of people in wheelchairs had come to be healed, but that's a whole other story.)

On the coffee-table altar, I placed pencil and paper. I asked Ruth to begin with an exploration in writing. We prayed together, affirming that she would leave the room a free woman.

I asked Ruth to draw a big circle in the middle of the sheet of paper and write in the circle everything she could think of that she held against her mother. "Take your time," I said. "It's important to get it all." After she was sure she had written it all, I asked three questions:

- Are you willing to forgive your mother completely, holding on to nothing?
- Are you willing to forgive her unconditionally—no excuses?
- Are you willing to forgive her such that you let go of all the stories about her that you have told yourself and others—not ever to speak or think negatively of her again?

Ruth nodded and said she was willing. To be willing is the miracle-working energy that opens the way for grace, for the activity of the power of release to do its work. Maybe Ruth by herself couldn't so profoundly release her mother, but God in her could and would. God in you will do the same for you.

Two more steps remained. I asked her to close her eyes and imagine her mother as a child standing before her. "Looking into your mother's eyes," I said, "is there something in your heart to say to her? Take a deep breath and, speaking from your heart, tell her what you want her to know—silently. And when you are done, open your eyes." As she did, I actually saw her face soften. I went on, "Please close your eyes again and, still looking into your mother's eyes, is there something she wants to say to you?" Tears began to roll down Ruth's cheeks. When she opened her eyes again, she said, "She told me she was sorry and that she loves me." Long pause as the tears flowed, then she spoke softly, "I'm not afraid now."

Only three months after this experience, Ruth died. I went to her home when I got the call of her passing. I was actually startled when I walked into her bedroom. Her face was radiant and on her lips was a beautiful smile. Divine release had cleared the way for the light of God to shine in her and out from her. I imagined that on the other side, her mother was waiting with a loving embrace.

Forgiveness is one of the many faces of the power of elimination. However, in a significant way, it is also a part of all that we choose to release. Whether we let go of a relationship, a job, a career, an attitude, a belief, a perception, a thought, an emotion, or a habit, our willingness to release begins with seeing that our peace, joy, and well-being are being diminished or totally blocked in one of those ways. Once we see it, the next step is to accept it as opposed to fighting it. In acceptance, there is the almost imperceptible fragrance of new freedom.

Rudy Garcia-Tolson was born with popliteal pterygium syndrome, a rare disease that left him with a club foot, webbed fingers on both hands, a cleft lip and palate, and the inability to straighten his legs. By the time he was 5, he had undergone 15—count 'em, 15—operations. At that tender age, he decided he would rather be a double amputee and walk with prosthetics than spend the rest of his days on the sidelines in a wheelchair. He released one hope—having normal legs—for another hope: to be able to participate in sports.

He began swimming at age 6. At age 8, he stated that he would swim in the 2004 Paralympic Games. He won a gold medal at 16! In 2008, he won the gold in the Beijing Paralympics. Swimming in the preliminaries at the 2012 Paralympics in London, he broke his own world record in the 200-meter Individual Medley.

Imagine all that he had to release from his thinking and emotions in order to embody a courageous, confident, championship consciousness. The power of elimination/release can and will empower you to live boldly from the indomitable spirit of God within you as, step-by-step, you release what isn't in the nature of the divine spirit within you.

Elimination is a spiritual solvent and also acts like spiritual acupuncture, in that it opens all the meridians of our being to the free flow of life, love, joy, and peace and the fulfillment of our highest potential.

Through the magic of social media, an old boyfriend from eighth grade reconnected with me. After all those years, there he was in the fourth row, stage right, in my Sunday morning service. I recognized him, even with a few more pounds and graying hair. We talked for a long time later in the day. He believed that his younger brother robbed him of his rightful inheritance. Though the experience was some 15 years earlier, he still hung on to it, blaming family members for his current financial problems. Instead of moving forward in his life, he tethered himself to the past. Instead of forgiving it all, he was still living it all. Instead of seeking the greatness in himself, he continued to seek the weaknesses in others. His "spiritual eraser" lay dormant, and he stood in unhappiness.

Conversely, Jim MacLaren, a world-renowned amputee tri-athlete, mastered his no-saying power. A handsome and accomplished Yale athlete, he was hit by a bus while riding his motorcycle home from school. One of his legs and, seemingly, his life was taken from him. Yet he made a choice to let go of the resentment and bitterness. He released the self-pity. He dug into the darkness and found the light in himself that was stronger than the darkness. He found a new dream. Step-by-step, positive thought by positive thought, he followed the light he could see into becoming a physically challenged Ironman triathlete, setting world records, doing what was thought impossible for amputees.

As if that weren't astounding enough, tragedy struck Jim's life again. He was hit by a van during the cycling portion of a triathlon in Orange County, California. This time he was left a quadriplegic. His spiritual power walked him into the light yet again. He became a motivational speaker who has inspired thousands of challenged athletes. Friends raised money to buy him a specially equipped van, giving him a modicum of freedom. As a result of the fund-raising, a community, a movement, and a new term were birthed—challenged athlete. Today the Challenged Athletes Foundation supports men and women to find and follow a new dream. This is the legacy of Jim MacLaren, who trained his mind to accentuate the positive and eliminate the negative.

The intentional spiritual practice of releasing what does not serve our well-being is a deep cleanser. As a deep facial cleanser extracts the impurities that clog the pores and age the skin, your spiritual cleanser extracts the impurities that clog the pores of your soul and limit your true freedom to experience unmitigated vitality, optimism, authentic relationship, and, let's face it, real happiness.

Another aspect of divine release is to let go of the fruits of your good efforts. Take quarterback Nick Mullens, an undrafted, second-year pro with the San Francisco 49ers. On November 1, 2018, Mullens stunned the crowd and the Oakland Raiders by setting NFL debut records to win 34-3 with 262 passing yards and three touchdowns. How did he do it? In an interview, Mullens said, "I just love football. Been playing since second grade. This is why you play, for stuff like this. When opportunities come along, you have to take advantage of them." His teammates said he out-practiced all of them. His coach said, "He gives 100 percent during every practice." To achieve what he did that day in November, his clear intention was to play his best and let go of the rest. He released everything except bringing all he knew to the present moment.

AFFIRM RELEASE

- *Divine elimination now cleanses me, spirit, soul, and body. I am made new.*

- *I release and let go of (fill in the blank) and focus on my heart's desires.*

- *I am willing to be and give my best and let go of the rest.*

VISUALIZE RELEASE

Take a deep, head-to-toe breath, bring your focus to your tailbone, and imagine an amber-colored light there. Watch it grow brighter and spiral up and down your body. See it sparkling as it circles through your legs into your feet and toes and up your torso, through your chest, shoulders, arms, hands, and fingers, up your neck and into your head. Breathe this shimmering light into every cell and atom of your being. Breathe it into your memories, confident that it will do its perfect cleansing work to set you free to live from your heart's desires and highest values.

PRAY RELEASE

God in me now releases and erases from my consciousness all that limits my happiness and well-being. I open to the activity of divine elimination now releasing my false beliefs. I give thanks that everything standing in the way of my usefulness to the people in my life and to life itself is removed. I focus on all that is beautiful, worthy, and worthwhile.

PRACTICE RELEASE

1. We can think our way into right acting or act our way into right thinking. Given that truth, begin by cleaning out one drawer a day for the next week. Then move to a closet. Give away or bring to consignment shops things you are no longer wearing. This prepares you to release the intangible, inner things that don't fit your best self and are out of style for the person you want to be.

2. Watch your thoughts and release those that are life/energy diminishing, unhelpful, and negative. Create two or three affirmations to say to fill the vacuum that release creates.

3. Give your best each day and let go of the outcomes. Live your present moments at your best.

REFLECT ON RELEASE

1. Consider a time when you released someone or something from your life. What did you see about the situation that empowered you to let go of the person, situation, or habit?

2. How do you know when it is time to stop doing what you have been doing, or to let go of someone or something you have been holding on to?

3. Without our *no*, our *yes* would lose its meaning and value. What are your thoughts about that?

Chapter 16

Zeal: Unstuck and Unstoppable

Zeal is the mighty force that incites the winds, the tides, the storms; it urges the planet on its course ... To be without zeal is to be without the zest of living. Zeal and enthusiasm incite to glorious achievement in every aim and ideal that the mind conceives. Zeal is the impulse to go forward.

—Charles Fillmore, *The Twelve Powers of Man*

My 9-year-old grandson Braedon was excited about our adventure to San Diego Zoo Safari Park. His eyes sparkled as he almost vibrated with enthusiasm. "I can't wait to see the elephants, lions, and giraffes!" he declared. As we walked along the winding pathways that sunny afternoon in Escondido, he spotted a huge yellow and royal blue hot-air balloon with people in it floating high above the park. He said, "I would never go on that—no way. Too scary. Would you, Gramma?" "I'd love to," I responded. He repeated, "Not me, never get me in that."

As we rode the Wild Animal Park tram around the perimeter, seeing the animals mostly from a distance, Braedon spotted the balloon again and asked, "Do you want to go up in the balloon, Gramma?" With great zeal, I answered, "Yes, I would just love to." He was quick to respond again, "Not me. No way." But clearly he was analyzing the possibility.

As our tram continued to circle the animal habitats, we could see the balloon continuing its ascent. Every couple of minutes,

Braedon would ask, "Do you still want to go in the balloon?" and I would repeat, "Yes, I would love to." As he continued to contemplate this daring adventure, he piped up, "It's getting dark and it's probably too late to go." Pause. "They probably closed it."

Yet when we came to the end of our tram ride, he bolted from the tram to see whether the balloon ride might still be open. Indeed, it was! I had caught up to him and the ride by now. "Can we go, Gramma?" he pleaded. "Of course," I replied and asked the operator of the ride if there was still time. "Yes, there sure is," he replied.

As it turned out, we were the only two on the ride. I was almost as excited as Braedon as we began to slowly ascend. As we rose, Braedon could only say, "I'm freaked," with a smile on his face. At about 50 feet up on the way to its 400-foot destination, all Braedon could say was how cool it was. Enthralled, he called his dad from his cell phone. "Dad, you should see where I am. Gramma and I are going up in a balloon. I can see all the animals! It's so cool."

When we descended back to ground level and stepped off, he was still uttering his new mantra, "That was so cool!" It was as if this little adventure was something he had wanted to do all his life—a dream come true. His fear had been transformed to rife enthusiasm.

In fact, his daring seemed to make a new "man" of him. And it does for us too. The power of spiritual zeal moves us up out of stuck conditions, mindsets, and self-defeating perceptions.

Spiritual zeal expresses enthusiasm and joy as well as courage, creative thinking, and commitment to a worthy cause. It is the affirmative impulse of life, ever seeking to move us forward. Seeded with the spiritual energy of the other powers, it can invigorate to accomplish what otherwise might seem impossible.

The zeal center resides at the nape of the neck. Pain in the neck could signal zeal out of balance. When we are trying to control or push our will, when we are impatient with people and circumstances, when we are pressing for a particular outcome, it might be that we are overzealous. While perseverance in pursuit of a heart's desire is one of the gifts of spiritual zeal, aggressive insistence is not.

This creative power vibrates the color orange—vibrant and stimulating. Not surprisingly, Simon the Zealot is a biblical representative for the power of zeal. The Jewish Zealots would not honor the gods of the Romans. They were, instead, passionate about living aligned with the commandments of Hebrew scripture. What might that mean for us today? It might look like being enthusiastic about life, about worthy goals. It might look like the kind of passion for something good that powers us through obstacles.

Virtuoso guitarist and composer Billy McLaughlin needed zeal in the midst of a heartbreaking time in his up-to-then successful career. He contracted a disease that limited his ability to play. For a while it seemed as if his whole life, identity, and creative expression were not only turned upside down, they were dismantled and locked away in a place he couldn't find. However, spiritual zeal was still alive in him. He reassembled his love of music and creative gift and found his way back home to himself, relearning to play the notes entirely on the neck of his guitar, using his right hand and two fingers of his left.

The vibrancy of his zeal seemed to pull him out of the darkness of loss and into the light. He mastered this new method of guitar playing. He created a new CD for acoustic guitar and string orchestra, *Into the Light*, in recognition of the light that had brought him out of the darkness.

Dante Alighieri described such an experience in *The Divine Comedy*. "In the middle of the journey of our lives, I came to myself in a dark wood where the direct way was lost." Most of us discover ourselves in that place at least once in our lives, as Billy McLaughlin did. Yet if we can touch what impassions us and invoke the power of zeal, light will trickle through the darkness to move us forward.

Charles Fillmore, a man of many endeavors and cofounder of Unity, found himself in a dark wood personally and professionally more than once. His experience in the dark led him on an intense spiritual search that resulted in a healing prayer ministry and his own miraculous healing. At 93, he still had the gusto to affirm in *Atom-Smashing Power of Mind*: *I fairly sizzle with zeal and enthusiasm and spring forth with a mighty faith to do the things that ought to be done by me.* He kept the power of zeal vibrantly activated by following his dreams. Zeal fuels our natural resilience.

Joseph of Panephysis writes, "Abba Lot went to Abba Joseph and said to him, 'Abba, as far as I can I say my little office, I fast a little, I pray and meditate, I live in peace and as far as I can, I purify my thoughts. What else can I do?' Then the old man stood up and stretched his hands toward heaven. His fingers became like ten lamps of fire and he said to him, 'If you will, you can become all flame.'"

Zeal is the flame that sets our hearts on fire with passion for the possible. It's the energy that inspires, motivates, energizes, and moves us forward to what we love and all that is important to us.

Take JT Holmes. He is what you would call a thrill-seeker. He does things that most of us would consider terrifying. People who know JT refer to him as humble and extraordinary at the same time. He is a professional skier, stuntman, motivational speaker, published writer, and nature lover. He has skydived off skyscrapers and mountain peaks. He has executed successful free-falls from city hotel rooftops. When asked, "Doesn't doing this stuff scare you?" JT responded, "Sure it does. I'm scared every day." Rather than stop him, however, feeling scared spurs him to the next adventure.

After allowing fear to stop me far too often, I made the same decision JT must have made. I realized that choosing to do things that scared me, turned my palms sweaty, and set my heart racing would, step-by-step, diminish fear in every area of my life.

Since then, I have bungee jumped from the 108th floor of the STRAT Hotel, Casino, and Skypod in Las Vegas (829 feet); jumped out of an airplane at 15,000 feet; and sat in a capsule that shot into the air at a force acceleration of 3Gs. Why? Because I came to understand that overcoming a fear in one area of my life affected *every* area of my life. Oddly enough, each time I felt closer to my God and more aligned with something in me that was greater than my fears. Spiritual zeal is always a contributing factor in such cases.

AFFIRM ZEAL

- *The passion of God fills my mind and heart, and I start to live my life as a great adventure.*

- *The passion in me sets me free to be all I've come here to be.*

- *Divine zeal now moves me forward to all that enlivens and empowers me.*

VISUALIZE ZEAL

Gently close your eyes; take a deep, long, enlivening breath. Imagine as you inhale that you are breathing in white light from the infinite resources of the Universe. Breathe this white light into the nape of your neck, the seat of divine zeal. In your mind's eye, watch the sparking orange light of divine zeal light up and expand to fill your whole body. Breathe zeal into every cell and atom, telling yourself that you are porous to the passion of God that makes you brilliantly creative, dynamically inspired, and fully equipped to manifest your heart's desires.

PRAY ZEAL

Most amazing God, thank you for kindling a passion for life in my heart so that I live each day as if it is my last, love as if I can't be hurt, and put my whole heart into all that I do to honor you and, at the same time, bless myself and others.

PRACTICE ZEAL

1. Do one thing each day that brings you joy.

2. Create a goal that energizes you just to think about it. Take one small step each day for the next week toward accomplishing it.

3. Wear something orange each day for two weeks.

REFLECT ON ZEAL

1. What brings you joy, and are you doing it?

2. What are you passionate about, and are you engaging with it in some way?

3. Is there a place in your life where you feel stuck? This is the place to pray for zeal—the courage to take action to become unstuck.

Chapter 17

Life: Naturally Creative

The world breaks every one and afterward many are strong at the broken places.

—Ernest Hemingway, *A Farewell to Arms*

Life is the faculty of movement, vitality, wholeness, and creativity. It is the expression of the pure, eternal life of God within us.

—*Metaphysics 2*

Nestled among art galleries in Santa Fe, New Mexico, the Frank Howell Gallery drew walkers in. The walls displayed his extraordinary paintings that captured the heart and soul of the people he studied. I wandered in there one day on a visit with my friend Brenda. I walked out of the gallery with three prints and two books of his vibrant art. In one of the books, couched next to a powerful painting of a Native-American medicine man, was a stirring meditation about the regenerating power of life by poet Nancy Wood. She wrote, "Pretend you are a newborn baby. Get the staleness of winter out of your heart, mind, and body. It's time to be reborn ... Regeneration means that you can start growing all over again, this time from the inside out. There is time for everything, even that which you thought too late to happen." (*Dancing Moons*, Doubleday, 1995)

This is a foundational principle of the power of life. A spiritual life demonstrates as creative expression, vitality, optimism, growth, and pristine moments of quiet regeneration. The divine presence within us is the life force of creativity. We see it every-where outside of us, even in flowers growing through rocks, but sometimes we miss the creativity that goes on inside of us. We are always creating because we are always thinking—whether awake or asleep—and thought is creative energy. Put another way, our thoughts create our experience. Think about this one: Everything in the visible world began as a thought.

The spiritual power of *life* is the very essence of the universe, the energy of all creation. It is the activity of the Spirit and Source of Life, called by many names. There is One Creative Force. It lives inside of us as well as outside of us. It is the matrix in which all form is born and sustained. It is the Invisible seeking visibility. In human beings, it is the creative urge as well as the energy of existence. It is the essence of all growth. It is the urge to expand our territory, as Jabez prayed in 1 Chronicles 4:10. It is the activity of progress, attainment, and mastery.

Life is the acting principle. Substance is the thing acted upon. Life is the energy that propels all form into action. Here's the key: It is raw, creative energy that requires directive power. That is our job. Therein lies the challenge and the gift. Let's consider:

Awe means to stand amazed before the amazing. Research on the power of awe has discovered surprising benefits. For exam-ple, moments of awe and wonder can not only take your breath away, they can reduce stress, enhance bonding, and improve your health. These moments light up something vitally alive in each of us. They give us life because they are so replete with life energy. Awe-deprived, we lose our creative edge and energy.

Judas, the biblical representative of the power of life, held a high vision for what Jesus would do to free people from Roman domination. He wanted Jesus to be a warrior and thought he could force Jesus into a power struggle with their enemies to prove it. It didn't work for Judas, and it doesn't work for us. Divine life is not creative in that way. Judas represents the spiritually undeveloped life forces, motivated largely by fear. When spiritually awakened and activated, the creative energy of life seeks loving, honorable ways to generate an increase of good.

Life vibrates red—just like our blood. As our blood pumps life into every part of our bodies, the divine power of life pumps energy into our hopes and dreams. Partnered with divine wisdom, we can be unstoppable in achieving all that matters most to us.

The energy of life is the foundation of our desires. The energy of life is not content with the status quo because its very nature is to create. Since we are cocreators with this Life Force, purifying the desires or motivations that arise from some form of fear is essential to our happiness and fulfillment.

Life is progress, attainment, and mastery. It is our innate desire to live fully alive. It is the urge to greater achievement. In *Jesus Christ Heals*, Charles Fillmore said, "The life source is spiritual energy. It is deeper and finer than electricity ... It is composed of ideas, and [we] can turn on its current by making mental contact with it."

I finally made mental contact with a vision that lay hidden on the back burners of my life for years. It came out of hiding to take first place on my bucket list recently. The vision that energized me was birthed in my high school Spanish class. Tucked in the middle of our textbook were heart-throbbing photos of Machu Picchu, Peru, with its verdant, cone-shaped peaks that seemed to touch the sky. The miracle of how the Incas managed to build an elaborate city 8,000 feet up the almost-vertical slopes tantalized my imagination and fueled my yearning to see this Wonder of the World firsthand.

Finally, years after high school, the seed planted then had taken root and now broke through the ground of my determination. Within six months of the breakthrough, I stood in that legendary city, looking out at those same cone-shaped peaks in utter awe. The views exceeded my highest flights of imagination. The inspiring views and this dream come true activated the creative energy of the life force in me beyond words. I tell this story to say that making our dreams come true, honoring the yearnings of our heart, gives expression to God as the life force in us. We are full of life when our dreams and our senses are fed.

Your life force engenders the power to draw from invisible substance the fulfillment of your highest ideas. Ideas of life working in and through the soul draw to you, from the four corners of the earth, the manifestation of what they represent. When divine life is expressing through you, it shows up as hope, optimism, enthusiasm, love, courage, strength, wisdom, and creative ideas.

Jerry had an extraordinary capacity to give life power not only to his day but to everyone he encountered. To the question, "Hi, Jerry. How are you?" he always had the same answer. Yet the same answer always sent a charge of energy to the receiver. His answer? "MAGNIFICENT!" Just like that—spoken in capital letters with an exclamation point. The power of life in him filled every syllable. If you knew Jerry, you would know that his life might not have looked so magnificent on the outside, but he refused to let that diminish his insides. He kept his connection to Source strong.

So did Louis Zamperini, a World War II veteran whose remarkable life came to light in Laura Hillenbrand's best-selling book *Unbroken* and then became an equally compelling movie of the same name. That's because Louis's life was a testament to the resilience of the human spirit, the power of the life force.

Born on January 26, 1917, he lived life to the fullest. You could say he was full of life, a light that could not be put out, even during 47 days in a raft at sea after his plane crashed into the ocean, even after he was captured, even while being tortured in Japanese prison camps. The experiences took their toll, but he worked his way out of depression and addiction to become a Christian evangelist. In his later years, still full of vibrant life, he devoted himself to working with at-risk youth.

When Louis passed away on July 2, 2014, at 97 years old, Random House took out a quarter page ad in *The New York Times* to honor him. At the top was a picture of an elderly Louis in his military uniform. There were the dates of his birth and death, but what followed told about the spirit of the man: OLYMPIAN, WORLD WAR II HERO, MAN OF FAITH, FRIEND. In color photographs, a radiance shines in his face, the radiance of the power of life fully alive and fully activated.

That same spirit of life lives in you and yearns to be maximized.

AFFIRM LIFE

- *The more I notice the beauty around me, the more the power of life expands within me.*

- *The more I do what brings me joy, the more I experience creative energy.*

- *The more I appreciate my life, the more life gives me to appreciate.*

VISUALIZE LIFE

Close your eyes gently; take a deep, long breath; and follow your breath down to the generative center of your body. As you focus your attention there, notice a brilliant red light appear. As you watch the sparkling red light, see it expand to fill your whole body, spiraling up and down, filling every cell and atom with its life-giving, creative energy. Breathe deeply and rest in this radiant light for a few moments, allowing the divine life force to renew, restore, rejuvenate, and regenerate you, spirit, soul, and body. Into this brilliant red light, ask the question: *What gives me life?* Listen for the "still, small voice" of Spirit within you to tell you. Listen for the revelation of what Spirit wants you to do to expand its energy and fulfill its purpose in you.

PRAY LIFE

Lord of life and all that is good and wholesome, inspiring and worthy, I give thanks that your life in me is newly awakened today in glorious ways. Thank you for enlightening my mind with new creative ideas, my spirit with new vigor, and my body with new energy. I give thanks that your life in me now dissolves anything unlike itself.

PRACTICE LIFE

1. Learn something new this year—a sport, a musical instrument, a game—something that interests you.

2. Spend time in beauty, whatever that might be for you.

3. Write down at least three things that are life-giving to you and do at least one this week.

REFLECT ON LIFE

1. What gives you life? Lights you up? Fires up your enthusiasm?

2. What are you giving life to these days? Same old, same old, or something that energizes you?

3. As you reflect on your life, what word or words summarize your endeavors?

Part Three

The Empowered Life

Chapter 18

Passion: The Fuel of Resilience

We must learn to watch our consciousness, its impulses and desires, as a chemist watches his solutions.

—Charles Fillmore, *The Twelve Powers of Man*

From the time my sister Nora and I played Elvis Presley or Louis Prima LPs and danced in our family room, I longed to make music. I didn't think I had it in me, though. Why? Because in the seventh grade at St. Juliana grade school in Chicago, we all had to sing in the choir. Maybe it was my own self-doubt and shyness, but I could swear the nun whispered to me one day, "Just mouth the words." That shut down any dreams of making music, let alone singing to the music.

Subsequently, with the yearning love of music in my heart, I heard a husband and wife duo playing mandolins on TV one evening. I asked my parents if I could take mandolin lessons. The answer was *no*. I only remember the *no*, not the reason, if there was one.

Discouraged but not despairing, my heart's desire to make music never left me. It was in the closet of my heart the whole time I was completing my education, forging a career, and raising my children.

Decades later, a friend invited me to join her at a concert at the Museum of Making Music in Carlsbad, California. I said *yes* instantly. As it turned out, all the musicians were amateurs. Most had played in high school and college and now, well into adult-hood, they had picked up where they left off. The closet door in my heart opened. At the conclusion of the concert, the conduc-tor invited the audience members to consider joining the group. She explained, "We have beginning, intermediate, and advanced groups. If you are interested, come up and talk to the musicians. We play on Wednesday evenings."

My heart sang at the possibility—after all these years. As peo-ple dispersed, I went to her. "I'm interested," I said. "Which is the easiest instrument?" She suggested, "The trumpet, trombone, or clarinet. Talk to one of the musicians. We'd love to have you join us." My heart pounding with hope, I spoke with the first chair clarinet player. She encouraged me. I think she may even have said, "It's not hard." I blocked out the voices of the past and the relentless inner worries that I didn't have what it takes to play a musical instrument. The next week I went to Bertrand's Music and rented a clarinet.

Now four years later, I'm in the intermediate band. I say this because willingness has been absolutely essential to my remain-ing in the band. There have been many moments while squeak-ing a high note that I've said to myself, *Give up. This doesn't come naturally to you.* Grace and willingness keep my heart open and my fingers practicing. My love of making music continually feeds my desire and endurance. It gives me the willingness to go on because I want to make music more than I don't want to practice. I want to empower my dreams, not my dread.

As author Michael Singer says in his book *The Untethered Soul,* we all have an inner roommate. It's that inner voice we can hear when we pay attention to our thoughts. It chatters away inces-santly, mostly outside of our awareness unless we know about it. I love the term Buddhists use—*monkey mind.* It screeches when we head toward a goal, a dream, or something that we have never tried. It gives bad advice. It stokes our fears. It cautions us, blames us, and scares us. Its whole motivation is safety and security—as fear would interpret it.

Our inner roommate lectures us on ways to be safe, not to change. It shakes its finger of fear, urging us to back away if there is no guarantee of a safe, easy passage, no guarantee of success. It exhorts us to get even, find fault, give up, or show them. If not recognized and treated, it can capture our whole attitude and outlook.

The good news is that it can be tamed. Why? Because it is not who we truly are. We are way more than our doubts, worries, and fears. Beyond that chatter is an awakened observer within us, one who can monitor our thoughts and feelings. Our observer self can change a fear-based, unhelpful thought in a nanosecond. We can learn to navigate through the vibrational turbulence our fears generate. Our observer can shift the focus to encouraging thoughts. It can remind us of the spark of divinity within us, igniting life-enhancing thoughts and feelings such as gratitude, appreciation, and compassion.

Our divine nature always trumps *monkey mind*. It shines through the 12 creative powers as they are spiritually developed.

We are always at a choice point—faith in God or faith in what tends to make us feel anxious. Fear or faith? Take your pick. Being willing to take action transforms blind faith into understanding faith. Understanding faith, in turn, generates more courageous right action.

Even knowing we were born with these 12 divine powers inherent in us, there are circumstances that wash up on the shores of our lives that create a crisis. Our current faith isn't big enough to handle the problem, pain, hurt, loss, difficulty, disappointment, or outrage. Negative emotions and thoughts erupt like an active volcano. Suddenly, we see obstacles on the path that appear insurmountable—or at least not worth the trip. Our forward momentum stalls.

Resilience doesn't take brilliance. What it takes is diligence and willingness to get up when you're down and to walk through the pain, knowing you will gain mastery. It's about your spiritual fitness and bearing witness to the radiant power of God in you.

Don't misunderstand me. Resilience is about being strong in more ways than one. It's about coming back when you get off track on the way to all the good you can do. It's about bouncing back when life takes you down, confident that the power of God in you will not let you drown in any sea of trouble but will make a way through and bless you while making you a blessing to others.

There is grace, divine empowerment, guidance, and support in being willing to act in the face of all the reasons why not.

Martin Luther King Jr. lived what he preached, despite the array of pitfalls on his quest for racial equality. He was willing to walk into the fray, empowered by his faith in God, his faith that light shines in every darkness and cannot be overcome by it. His willingness, arising from his faith, empowered his first step and every courageous step after that. His willingness graced his journey as he changed the course of history.

Willingness, in some mystical and miraculous way, puts a demand on the Universe. It seems to reach into the heart of God and draw to us the power not only to demonstrate resilience in the face of losses, disappointments, and seeming failure but the perseverance to follow our hopes and dreams. It diminishes our fears with each step we take so that our natural radiance shines more power on our path. We step out of the dark and into the light of new beginnings.

AFFIRM

- *I let go of monkey-mind thoughts and focus on positive possibilities.*

- *I awaken my observer self and take dominion over my thoughts and actions.*

- *Spirit in me makes me a possibility thinker and doer.*

PRAY

Opulent giver of life and architect of the cosmos and our most beautiful dreams, you are the radiance of the universe and of my heart, ever singing your extraordinary possibilities into my thoughts. I open my mind and heart to the fragrance of your presence, willing to persevere and, even more, to thrive in the midst of any challenge. I step out in faith to follow my bliss.

VISUALIZE

Gently close your eyes as you take a deep, long breath into the fullness of your own presence, which is within the divine presence. The divine presence is your power to live a graced life. The spirit of love, wisdom, beauty, strength, order, and all goodness are alive in you. Remind your heart that you are never alone. Imagine being equipped to do and experience all that your heart desires—for yourself, your loved ones, and our world. Light your imagination with technicolor pictures. What would a graced life look like to you? How would you be putting your faith into action? Rest in all the beautiful pictures that you can create and all the enlivening feelings you experience. Tell yourself, *My life is graced because I put my faith into action.*

PRACTICES

1. For the next 21 days, do one thing each day that brings you joy.

2. This week, pull out a dream that has lived on the back burners of your mind and do one small thing to give it life (such as take a dance lesson, go skydiving, ice skate, or write a poem).

3. Reflect on all of the brave things you have done—don't minimize! Let this energize you for step two.

Chapter 19

The Rewards of Discipline: Spiritual Mastery

Unspeakable joy, glory, and eternal life are promised to those who with unselfish devotion strive to develop [a spiritualized] consciousness. All the glories of the natural man are as nothing compared with the development of the spiritual man.

—Charles Fillmore, *The Twelve Powers of Man*

L ooking out the six-foot arched windows of my office at the remains of a winter ice storm, the trees were glistening crystals—monuments to the power of the universe and its capacity to change the environment totally. You and I have been given that same awesome power to change our inner environment by the Source of all power. We can change our minds, and a change in conditions will follow as surely as day follows night and spring follows winter.

Springtime lives in every cell and atom of our bodies, full of life and vitality, ready to blossom into luxurious experiences, fragrant with happiness. It's there in boundless potential in the fields of our consciousness. It's there even though we may not see it or feel it. A rich, fertile life, blossoming with beauty and deliciousness, rises from the soil of a consciousness that has been well-fertilized with spiritual nutrients.

These 12 powers are the spiritual nutrients that generate miracle-mindedness so that we not only see miracles all around us, but we also become magnetic to miracles. We are empowered to create a life we love, one that is fulfilling, meaningful, and impactful. We become a spiritual presence that blesses everyone and everything around us.

When Jesus was transfigured high on a mountain in the presence of disciples Peter, James, and John, he was demonstrating the full development of these 12 powers. Later when he walked out of the tomb, he reconstructed his body through fully igniting the power of the 12 and entered a new dimension of living. So can you and I. Right here on earth, the joy of heaven can be expressed as, in, and through you and me.

In his letter to the Ephesians, who were waffling in their faith, Paul promised that if they would commit to establishing a spiritual fitness program, they would mature spiritually to the point where their consciousness would be transformed and they would "no longer be children, tossed to and fro and blown about by every wind" of circumstances in their lives and the opinions of others (Ephesians 4:14). They would be empowered to live a life beyond their highest flights of imagination.

Henry David Thoreau described this kind of life in *Walden*, saying, "If one advances confidently in the direction of his dreams, and endeavors to live the life which he has imagined, he will meet with a success unexpected in common hours. He will put some things behind, will pass an invisible boundary; new, universal, and more liberal laws will begin to establish themselves around and within him; or the old laws be expanded, and interpreted in his favor in a more liberal sense, and he will live with the license of a higher order of beings."

As you continue to develop your 12 spiritual powers, you will put some ways of being behind and experience all the promises Thoreau experienced.

Charles Fillmore described the outcome of a life committed to spiritual practice and growth as crossing an invisible boundary into the "fourth dimension." He called it living in the kingdom of heaven—now. It is cleansing our hearts and minds and discovering we intuitively know how to handle situations that used to baffle us. We see through appearances and don't judge by them. Rather than react to circumstances, we respond effectively from spiritual principle. Our thinking is more and more on a plane of inspiration. We develop a sixth sense that is a reliable guide to right action.

When I moved to Gainesville, Florida, I looked for a fitness center to join. I wanted to be in peak physical condition and knew I'd need to work with a trainer to accomplish that. I found just the right one. Wade Cleary was more than up to the task. He was a strapping young college student. His muscular body was evidence of his committed discipline to the practice. During our sessions, I would moan and groan, pleading, "Please, no more slow reps!" I got no sympathy from him. He would push me to press more weight than I thought possible. I'd groan and he'd say, "One more, one more. C'mon, you can do this!" He once told me it was essential to push the muscle until it couldn't go any further—to the breaking point—in order to get to the next level of fitness. That, he said, was the way to bring the muscle to its peak performance level—like a finely tuned engine, like a Stradivarius violin.

The same is true for these 12 spiritual muscles. The more we work them in the difficult circumstances of our lives, the more powerful and effective they become. When life seems to take us to the breaking point, we find that the spiritual power we have built up is doing for us what we could not do on our own. We come to know a new freedom and a new peace.

When I lived in San Francisco, I attended a weekend workshop offered by the renowned master of sound healing, Jill Purce. What she could do with her voice was astounding—her toning climbed up and down octaves. The practice was exhilarating, and I know it was healing. Jill said, "If the voice is liberated, the human is liberated."

The same is true about practicing these 12 powers through praying them, visualizing them in your body, studying their spiritual expression, wearing the colors of each power, and calling on them in times of need as well as in times of peace and joy. When we liberate them, we liberate ourselves.

Tending to our spiritual growth is to answer the yearning and call of the One who is the life of our life. It is the call to enter the unknown and become fully known.

St. Scholastica Academy stood tall and proud on Ridge Boulevard in Chicago, about a mile from the shores of Lake Michigan. I spent four years of high school there in the company of almost 900 girls, more than 70 Benedictine nuns, and occasional guest priests. The school was separated from the Benedictine Motherhouse (the place where novices are trained, nuns are housed, and the elderly retire and are cared for) by one doorway on each of the three floors. The first-floor doorway led to the kitchen, laundry, infirmary, and offices. The second-floor doorway led to the chapel and beyond the chapel to another door, always closed, to the nuns' quarters. Beyond the third-floor doorway was pure mystery. None of us, except those girls who decided to enter the convent, ever got beyond that door.

We could go to the chapel anytime, however, and be in the mystery, silence, and energy of a hundred years of Benedictine chanting, prayer, and incense. We went for chapel services once a week and on special holidays. Passing silently through the second-floor doorway, we entered the double doors of the sanctuary and into a kind of silence that awakened my heart and almost took my breath away. In the mystery of this marble and stained glass holy place, surrounded by heavenly paintings, little side altars, marble columns, and larger-than-life statues of Mary, Jesus, Joseph, St. Scholastica, and St. Benedict, with dozens of flickering candles before them, you could almost taste the presence of God, the Unnameable Mystery.

I mention all this because there is a holy mystery about these 12 spiritual powers. While each has its practical, human expression, each also has a spiritual dimension that is both practical and mysterious. These powers have life, substance, and intelligence. They are power itself. They know what to do beyond what we know.

The famous Road to Hana on Maui, Hawaii, boasts 617 hairpin curves. Life is sometimes like that—lots of unexpected curves. You could experience a death, loss of a job, loss of a relationship, divorce, empty nest, or financial setbacks. Life can change on a dime. That is why it's so important to maintain our spiritual fitness. Developing the 12 spiritual powers will be a key for you to achieve optimum spiritual well-being.

Vincent van Gogh wrote in a letter, "For the great doesn't happen through impulse alone, and is a succession of little things that are brought together." A succession of moments given to their development yields great rewards. It parallels mastering anything— playing an instrument, improving your tennis or golf game, or working out at the gym. A skill is a skill.

Our spiritual journey seems to require that our faith be tested over and over. Maybe our faith in the power of God in us and all around us can only grow when tested by life. Courage is just a word until we act from it when we are afraid. Our love and compassion grow when the difficulty of resentment and judgment are overcome.

That's part of our inherent resilience—the capacity to rise out of deadening, life-depleting, scary circumstances. It is the innate capacity to shift from hate to forgiveness, from fear to courage, from victim to victor, from blame to personal responsibility. With commitment to practicing spiritual principles and praying and living from the 12 powers, we will light up a room with our radiance. We will have surrendered who we are not for who we really are in our heart and soul—a light in the world.

AFFIRM

- *I focus my thoughts on what gives me life and brings me joy.*

- *I take time to notice the good and beautiful and appreciate it out loud.*

- *I let my light shine by loving courageously, living fully, and laughing easily.*

PRAY

In this moment, I release vestiges of small living, fenced love, and limited believing. I welcome the mantel of Spirit in me, making me braver still for the depths and heights and breadths of living and love. I court my soul's truest hunger and thirsts with gratitude and happy expectation.

VISUALIZE

Take a deep, full breath as you walk your mind into your inner sanctuary. Breathe deep and come into the pristine silence with your full attention. Come rest your mind in the rhythm of your deep breathing, envisioning the light of God filling every cell, every bone and muscle with radiant life and vitality. Rest your heart in peace-producing visions of good. Envision the best and let go of the rest. Envision bringing your best to the day.

PRACTICE

1. As you come to know the powers and colors, pay attention to the colors you choose to wear. Choose colors of the powers you want to cultivate.

2. Pay attention to the colors you choose for your home, office, and car. What colors are enlivening? What accent colors match the powers that are most supportive and empowering at this time in your life? I once didn't like the color red. It was almost offensive to my sensibilities. Eventually, I discovered that my upbringing did not permit me to acknowledge hurt and anger. Once I could accept and acknowledge my anger, a whole new world of freedom and life opened to me. I now wear red and have many red accents in my home. I appreciate and am grateful for the power of life.

3. In your prayer and meditation times, breathe the color of the powers throughout your body. Acknowledge to yourself that these divine energies are ministering to you. They are. You are building spiritual power that will come to your aid in times of need.

4. Create affirmations for the powers you want to expand and amplify. As you read earlier, one of my affirmations for a couple of years was, *My capacity to give and receive love increases dramatically*. It came out of being told that I wasn't a very good friend. It hurt my heart to hear that. I wanted to be loving, so I made that affirmation a mantra. Honestly, it began to work. I actually found myself feeling and being more loving.

Chapter 20

The Provenance of Your Greatest Contribution

Bear in mind that there is not a moment in which your character is not being shaped in one direction or another, and that your life is simply the product of repeated choices. Grandeur of character is the effect of many habits. Know precisely what you want, proceed directly to it, and the best results will reward your diligence.

—Grenville Kleiser, *Inspiration and Ideals*

In the middle of winter I at last discovered that there was in me an invincible summer.

—Albert Camus, "Return to Tipasa"

The pier in Oceanside, California, extends out 100 feet into the water. Ruby's Diner is perched at the very end of the pier. That was our dinner destination. Ruby's is a funky throwback to the 1950s. The views are extraordinary and the sunsets magnificent.

As my friend Helen and I walked along, we passed fishermen on both sides of the pier, patiently waiting for a bite. What captured our attention was a young boy, maybe four feet tall, standing shoulder to shoulder with the adults. The adults' lines were not bobbing at all. Yet this young boy was catching fish as fast as he could take one off the line, rebait, and throw the line back in. He was an irresistible fish attractor—as if he were one of those glow sticks luring the fish to his line.

What we have learned about how the universe operates is that every object in the universe releases light. To be in the universe is to release light. The young boy catching all the fish must have been emitting light. Maybe it was his passion for fishing. Maybe it was his faith, expecting to catch fish. Maybe it was his imagination picturing himself catching fish. Probably without even realizing it, he emitted a radiance that arose from his love of fishing and his dedication to the art of fishing at Oceanside Pier.

Our inherent passion for the possible is the divine presence in us seeking to express its light. We already have all the nascent power we need to create the life we dream of, to be the empowered person we were born to be, to fish in the ocean of all possibility with the same kind of prosperity that the curly-haired young boy demonstrated.

How bright our light shines depends on nurturing it into its highest wattage through our spiritual practice. Jesus assured us this is possible. We can do it through maturing and expressing it in the 12 essential ways you've read about here.

The call to be a light in our world lives in our heart and soul and forever invites us to plug into the One Great Light and to be part of creating a world that works for all. Like the boy on the pier attracting fish to his lure, as we master life's challenges by developing our spiritual powers, we attract experiences that feed us, spirit, soul, and body—and we do light up our world.

Up-leveling our 12 divine attributes to their full spiritual expression makes us a bright, inspiring, healing light in our world. There is a healing radiance about us. Our radiance is the peace and joy of Spirit vibrantly expressing as us.

The journey to find our true purpose, one that can contain all the ups and downs, the disappointments and discouragement, the drive and passion, calls us to the highest possible intentions for living. At the same time, life continually tests the human expression of our 12 powers. We can experience crises in faith. Our imaginations can picture worst-case scenarios rather than our purest heart's desires fulfilled. All of it is grist for the mill of developing the divine seed within us. We can use our difficulties not to slow us but to lift us and grow us.

Jesus said, "You are the light of the world ... Let your light shine before others, so that they may see your good works and give glory to your Father in heaven" (Matthew 5:14, 16).

It doesn't take some extraordinary feat to make a powerful difference. A listening heart, a kind gesture, a helping hand, or a word of appreciation—these can change another's life forever for the better. There are thousands of ways to make a difference, and each one has its impact on the whole body we call humanity. At the same time, each one arises from having tapped into a spiritual aspect of one of our 12 powers.

Meister Eckhart, the Christian monk and mystic, said, "The seed of God is in us ... Now the seed of a pear tree grows into a pear tree, a hazel seed into a hazel tree, the seed of God into God." It is an adventure in maturing our inherent resilience into a light that shines in the world. We emit radiance.

The seed of God is in us. It is the great work and the great adventure in our lives to grow that inherent resilience from seed into radiance—the radiance of peace, joy, and healing presence. That is where the bliss is.

Acknowledgments

This book has been many years in gestation, 35 to be exact, when in my first years as a ministerial student, the brilliant Rev. Marvin Anderson shared his passion for the 12 powers. My own passion was ignited and has remained through all these years. Thank you, thank you, Marvin.

I also keep close in my heart with deep gratitude:

> My beloved friends Sheryl Hodgins, Mary Ellen Jirak, and Rhonda Ceccato for their enthusiasm and support for this project

> The Unity ministers who invited me to present a 12 powers workshop in their ministries

> The late Neal Vahle, who was my sounding board for writing all these years

> The amazing, innovative Norm Shealy, M.D., Ph.D., for believing in the project and supporting me in this undertaking

> The incredible Larry Dossey, M.D., whose friendship has been a huge blessing, whose writing inspires me, and whose sharing on resilience energized my own

> Rev. Ellen Debenport, my awesome editor at Unity Books, whose keen, crisp questions and suggestions provoked and clarified my thinking

Bibliography

A Beautiful Mind, Universal Pictures, 2001.

Behrend, Genevieve, *Your Invisible Power: Working Principles and Concrete Examples in Applied Mental Science*, School of Builders, Inc., New York, 1921.

Butterworth, Eric, *Discover the Power Within You*, HarperSanFrancisco, San Francisco, 1968.

Camus, Albert, "Return to Tipasa," *The Myth of Sisyphus and Other Essays*, Vintage International, New York, 1983, pp. 193-204.

Carroll, Lewis, *Alices's Adventures in Wonderland and Through the Looking-Glass and What Alice Found There*, Penguin Books, New York, 1998.

Coelho, Paulo, *The Alchemist* by Paulo Coelho. Copyright (c) 1988 by Paulo Coelho. English translation copyright (c) 1993 by Paulo Coelho and Alan R. Clarke. Used by permission of HarperCollins Publishers.

Cope, Stephen, *The Great Work of Your Life: A Guide for the Journey to Your True Calling*, Bantam Books, New York, 2012.

The Curious Case of Benjamin Button, Paramount Pictures, 2008.

Fillmore, Charles, *Atom-Smashing Power of Mind*, Unity Books, Unity Village, Mo., 1949.

———, *Christian Healing: The Science of Being*, 10th ed., Unity Books, Unity Village, Mo., 1922.

———, *Jesus Christ Heals*, Unity Books, Unity Village, Mo., 1955.

———, *Keep a True Lent*, Unity Books, Unity Village, Mo., 1957.

———, *Prosperity*, 3rd ed., Unity Books, Unity Village, Mo., 1938.

———, *The Revealing Word*, Unity Books, Unity Village, Mo., 1955.

———, *The Twelve Powers of Man*, Unity Books, Unity Village, Mo., 1930.

Fillmore, Cora, *Christ Enthroned in Man*, Unity Books, Unity Village, Mo., 1937.

Foner, Philip S. (ed.), *The Complete Writings of Thomas Paine*, The Citadel Press, New York, 1945, Vol. II.

Grant, Rubin E., "'I Just Love Football': Mullens Making the Most of His Opportunity with the 49ers," *Over the Mountain Journal*, August 19, 2019,<https://www.otmj.com/nick-mullens-49ers/>, accessed on May 26, 2020.

Hausmann, Winifred Wilkinson, *Your God-Given Potential*, Unity Books, Unity Village, Mo., 1978.

Hemingway, Ernest, *A Farewell to Arms*, Scribner, New York, 2014.

John XXIII, *Journal of a Soul*, Image Books, New York, 1999.

Keller, Helen, *The Story of My Life*, Doubleday, Page & Co., New York, 1903.

Kleiser, Grenville, *Inspiration and Ideals: Thoughts for Every Day*, 3rd ed., Funk & Wagnalls, New York, 1918.

Levy, Daniel S., "Santiago Calatrava," *Time*, April 18, 2005, < http:// content.time.com/time/specials/packages/article/0,28804, 1972656_1972696_1973384,00.html>, accessed on May 26, 2020.

Merton, Thomas, *New Seeds of Contemplation* by Thomas Merton, copyright ©1961 by The Abbey of Gethsemani, Inc . Reprinted by permission of New Directions Publishing Corp.

Metaphysics 2: The Fundamental Teachings of Unity, Unity Books, Unity Village, Mo., 1989.

Meichenbaum, Donald, "Important Facts About Resilience: A Consideration of Research Findings About Resilience and Implications for Assessment and Treatment," The Melissa Institute.

Myss, Caroline, *Anatomy of the Spirit: The Seven Stages of Power and Healing*, Penguin Random House, New York, 1997.

————, *Entering the Castle: An Inner Path to God and Your Soul*, Free Press, New York, 2007.

Newberg, Andrew, et al., *Why God Won't Go Away: Brain Science and the Biology of Belief*, Ballantine, New York, 2001.

Nin, Anaïs, *Seduction of the Minotaur*, Swallow Press, Chicago, 1961.

Oman, Maggie (ed.), *Prayers for Healing: 365 Blessings, Poems, and Meditations from Around the World*, Conari Press, Berkeley, 1999.

Perkins, John, *Shapeshifting: Techniques for Global and Personal Transformation*, Destiny Books, Rochester, Vt., 1997.

Pomeroy, Ella, *Powers of the Soul: And How to Use Them*, Island Press, New York, 1948.

Rampersad, Arnold, and David Roessel (eds.), *The Collected Poems of Langston Hughes*, Knopf, New York, 1994.

Rouse, Mick, "How JT Holmes Psyches Himself Up for Death-Defying Stunts," *The Edit Express*, <https://www.express.com/blog/people-we-love/how-jt-holmes-psyches-himself-up-for-death-defying-stunts>, accessed on June 12, 2020.

Schuller, Robert H., *Reach Out for New Life*, Bantam Books, Toronto, 1979.

Schultz, Charles, *Peanuts*, August 28, 1977.

Scioli, Anthony, and Henry B. Biller, *The Power of Hope: Overcoming Your Most Daunting Life Difficulties—No Matter What*, Health Communications, Inc., Deerfield Beach, Fla., 2010.

Seneca, *De Providentia*, quoted by Carlin A. Barton, *Roman Honor: The Fire in the Bones*, Univ. of California Press, Berkeley, 2001.

Singer, Michael A., *The Untethered Soul: The Journey Beyond Yourself*, New Harbinger Publications, Inc., Oakland, 2007.

Thoreau, Henry David, *Walden*, Ticknor and Fields, Boston, 1854.

Tolstoy, Leo, *My Reply to the Synod's Edict of Excommunication*, quoted by Edward A. Thurber, "Tolstoy's Religion," *The Open Court*, January 1914, pp. 1-12.

Von Drehle, David, et al., "How Do You Forgive a Murder?" *Time*, November 23, 2015, <https://time.com/time-magazine-charleston-shooting-cover-story/>, accessed on May 26, 2020.

Ward, Benedicta, *The Sayings of the Desert Fathers: The Alphabetical Collection*, Cistercian Publications, Kalamazoo, Mich., 1975.

Whyte, David, "Coleman's Bed," *River Flow: New and Selected Poems, 1984-2007*, Many Rivers Press, Langley, Wash., 2007, pp. 288-289.

Wood, Nancy, *Dancing Moons*, Doubleday, New York, 1995.

———, *The Heart Aroused: Poetry and the Preservation of the Soul in Corporate America*, Currency, New York, 1994.

———, *The House of Belonging*, Many Rivers Press, Langley, Wash., 1997.

About the Author

Rev. Sharon Connors is a Unity minister who has served ministries in Florida, San Francisco, San Diego, and Unity Village Chapel at Unity World Headquarters in Missouri. At this printing, she serves Unity Spiritual Center of Sun City, Arizona.

She has served on the board of trustees for Unity Worldwide Ministries as well as on Unity regional boards and community boards of directors. Sharon is a certified life coach specializing in personal growth, leadership development, and executive presence. In addition to her books, Sharon's articles have been published in *Daily Word®*, *Unity Magazine®*, and local newspapers.

She earned a bachelor's degree in Spanish and education from Michigan State University and a master's in vocational counseling from Northeastern Illinois University. In addition, she is a certified handwriting analyst and a certified Conversational Leadership facilitator.

Other Books by Sharon Connors

Adventures in Prayer: Praying Your Way to a God You Can Trust (Bantam, 2004)

Adventures in Prayer: The Magic of Discovery: Find the Treasures in You and the Gifts of Prayer for children (WestBow Press, 2010)

Seasons of Inspiration journal (Prayer Frontiers, 2012)

B0185